HOW THE STOCK MARKET WORKS

The Daily Telegraph

HOW THE STOCK
MARKET
WORKS

a beginner's guide to investment

2nd edition

MICHAEL BECKET

theshare centre:

KOGAN
PAGE

If you speculate on the stock market, you do so at your own risk.

First published in 2002
Reprinted in 2002, 2003
Second Edition, 2004
Reprinted in 2005, 2006, 2007

Kogan Page Limited
120 Pentonville Road
London N1 9JN
United Kingdom
www.kogan-page.co.uk

© Michael Becket, 2002, 2004

British Library Cataloguing in Publication Data

A CIP record for this book is available from the British Library.

ISBN-10   0 7494 4190 9
ISBN-13   978 0 7494 4190 6

Typeset by Saxon Graphics Ltd, Derby
Printed and bound in Great Britain by Bell & Bain, Glasgow

Contents

Contents

Trading shares now costs just £1.50 a go.

There's now a new way to get into the stock market... Halifax ShareBuilder. It's an online, monthly savings plan that lets you buy shares in virtually all UK listed companies for just £1.50 per deal! Now you can play the markets with as little as £20 per month. To learn more about Halifax ShareBuilder, just call **0845 850 5595**.

HALIFAX Always giving you extra

Contents _____

Preface

Investing demands some work, if only to have a standard for checking advice from professionals. It has been difficult enough to acquire the money so it would be silly not to put in a little more effort to ensure it is well used. That does not mean an investigation followed by a once-and-for-all decision about where to put the cash, but some monitoring of how it is performing and what the alternatives are. That applies to shares as well because stock markets change continuously. Everything about them is volatile and affected by a fierce entrepreneurial spirit.

The most obvious and continuously-reported change is market sentiment. That in turn is influenced by the changing prospects for exchange rates, by fluctuations in economies, as well as by profits and share prices. They all affect and can transform trading, sometimes producing passing blips and sometimes long-term swoops of market attitudes.

Old hands know that a longish period of depressed share prices makes investors worried there will be no upturn in the foreseeable future and there is no point in investing in the market. They then look to other homes for savings, such as art, antiques, fine wines, property to let, bonds, gold, or even commodities. Yes, they know that for the past hundred years or so, the stock market has outperformed almost every other investment – though you have to be careful about the period of comparisons – but they get nervous that this time the underlying circumstances might just have changed. There are always some soothsayers to tell them so. Perhaps the pattern has been broken by the changed economic conditions. But the cycle turns, those other investments turn out not to be infallibly successful, and when savers look again they realize share prices can go up as well as down.

Of course the converse of all that holds with equal force. Long periods of soaring share prices fool people into thinking it is a one-way bet and they cannot lose almost irrespective of where they put the money. Then there is a reaction, which is almost invariably overdone, and people wail about lost money and having been defrauded or mis-sold.

That is only of the aspects of change. These are the most visible and sometimes the most traumatic changes but there are other alterations, though some of those are those knock-on effects. It does however mean that a book like this needs to give varied warnings. Inexperienced people venturing into shares need to be made wary that when share prices have slumped, it is not merely the end of the world – it may be good news in disguise. For example, the loss in investment value is only notional unless you have to sell the shares. That is an argument for either extremely knowledgeable continuous trading or as warning to invest only for the medium to long term. It may also be an opportunity for finding the bargains others have shunned in the fear of a long slump.

Conversely, when the market is booming the warning is not get carried away with enthusiasm in the confident expectation it does not matter what you buy because it will be twice as expensive next week. Small investors cannot afford to take major gambles and are obliged to stick to value – that applies whether you are buying a tiny company which has been neglected but could grow very fast, or sticking to nice and safe blue chips.

Another aspect of the change is in the structure of the market and what is available in it. Sectors wax and wane with the external demand for their goods and services, the changes in ownership and the international structure. New securities appear regularly. A decade back and venture capital trusts or securitized property would have been unknown. Those clever financiers are constantly inventing new forms of derivatives, some of which are out-and-out gambles, while others provide a better spread of investment targets or greater security.

On top of that the market itself changes. For example, the London stock exchange is spreading into Continental shares by starting to trade in Dutch shares at a cost 40 per cent lower than the fees charged by Euronext. Euronext – which is the unified system for the exchanges in Amsterdam, Paris, Brussels and Lisbon – retaliated by trading in some UK shares and has promised to undercut the London exchange in its fees. The German stock exchanges, Deutsche Börse, then joined the fight by setting up their own trading in Dutch shares.

The reason for the fight in the dealing of Dutch shares is the presence of large international companies whose shares are widely held beyond the borders of the Netherlands: eg Philips, Unilever, Royal Dutch (which is the Dutch half of the Shell group), plus several big banks. Similar qualities exist for the London market, which means the fight could well intensify for customers in those shares. This can only be good for investors as the fees are likely to come down all round but it will take time to see how much it helps small investors.

All those reasons meant it was time for a second, updated edition of the book, to keep pace with the changes.

Acknowledgements

I am grateful to Kay Broadbent for reading through this, to help get it a bit more right and useful, and for her advice, which I occasionally followed. The mistakes of omission and commission are despite her best efforts, and are mine alone.

I would also like to thank Jasmin Smith of the Stock Exchange for going through the book to remove a number of mistakes.

What this book is about

Investing demands some work, if only to have a check against which to judge advice from professionals. It has been difficult enough to acquire the money, so it would be silly not to put in a little more effort to ensure it is well used. That does not mean an investigation followed by a once-and-for-all decision about where to put the cash, but some monitoring of how it is performing and what the alternatives are. That applies to shares as well, because stock markets change continuously. Everything about them is volatile and affected by a fierce entrepreneurial spirit.

The most obvious and continuously reported change is market sentiment. That in turn is influenced by the changing prospects for exchange rates, by fluctuations in economies, as well as by profits and share prices. They all affect and can transform trading, sometimes producing passing blips and sometimes long-term swoops of market attitudes.

Old hands know that a longish period of depressed share prices makes investors worried there will be no upturn in the foreseeable future – and there is no point in investing in the market. They then look to other homes for savings, such as art, antiques, fine wines, property to let, bonds, gold, or even commodities. Yes, they know that for the past hundred years or so, the stock market has outperformed almost every other investment – though you have to be careful about the period of comparisons – but they get nervous that this time the underlying circumstances might just have changed. There are always some soothsayers to tell them so, perhaps the pattern has been broken by the changed economic conditions. But the cycle turns, those other investments turn out not to be infallibly successful, and when savers look again they realize share prices can go up as well as down.

And of course the converse of all that holds with equal force. Long periods of soaring share prices fool people into thinking it is a one-way bet and they cannot lose almost irrespective of where they put the money. Then there is a reaction, which is almost invariably overdone, and people wail about lost money and having been defrauded or mis-sold.

That is only one of the aspects of change. These are the most visible and sometimes the most traumatic changes, but there are other alterations, though some of those are those knock-on effects. It does however mean that a book like this needs to give varied warnings. Inexperienced people venturing into shares need to be made aware that when share prices have slumped, it is not only not the end of the world, it may be good news in disguise. For example, the loss in investment value is only notional unless you have to sell the shares. That is either an argument for extremely knowledgeable continuous trading or a warning to invest only for the medium to long term. It may also be an opportunity for finding the bargains others have shunned in the fear of a long slump.

Conversely, when the market is booming the warning is do not get carried away with enthusiasm in the confident expectation that it does not matter what you buy because it will be twice as expensive next week. Small investors cannot afford to take major gambles and are obliged to stick to value – that applies whether you are buying a tiny company which has been neglected but could grow very fast, or sticking to nice and safe blue chips.

Another aspect of the change is in the structure of the market and what is available in it. Sectors wax and wane with the external demand for their goods and services, the changes in ownership and the international structure. New securities appear regularly. A decade back and venture capital trusts or securitized property would have been unknown. Those clever financiers are constantly inventing new forms of derivatives, some of which are out-and-out gambles, while others provide a better spread of investment targets or greater security.

On top of that the market itself changes. For example, the London Stock Exchange is spreading into Continental shares by starting to trade in Dutch shares at a cost 40 per cent lower than the fees charged by Euronext. Euronext – the unified system for the exchanges in Amsterdam, Paris, Brussels and Lisbon – retaliated by trading in some UK shares and has promised to undercut the London exchange in its fees. The German stock exchanges, Deutsche Börse, then joined in the fight by setting up their own trading in Dutch shares.

The reason for the fight in the dealing of Dutch shares is the presence of large international companies whose shares are widely held beyond the borders of Holland: eg Philips, Unilever, Royal Dutch (the Dutch half of the Shell group), plus several big banks. Similar qualities exist for the London market, which means the fight could well intensify for customers in those shares. This can be only good for investors, as the fees are likely to come down all round, but it will take time to see how much it helps small investors.

All these reasons meant it was time for a second, updated edition of the book, to keep pace with the changes.

Some warnings:

Anyone who thinks there is safety in numbers hasn't read the stock market page.
Irene Peter

Do not bother to sell your Gas shares. The electric light has no future.
Professor H Pepper (1821–1900)

An unnecessary collection of low fellows who speculate in the Funds and are of no benefit to anyone but themselves.
Dr Johnson (on stockbrokers)

There is no moral difference between gambling at cards or in lotteries or on the racetrack, and gambling in the stock market. One method is just as pernicious to the body politic as the other kind, and in degree the evil worked is far greater.
Theodore Roosevelt, message to Congress, 31 January 1908

The way to make money on the Exchange is to sell too soon.
Nathan Rothschild

One must get into the market as into a cold bath – quick in and quick out.
Solomon Rothschild (1774–1855)

Buy good securities, put them away, forget them.
Timothy Bancroft

October is one of the peculiarly dangerous months to speculate on stocks in. The others are July, January, September, April, November, May, March, June, December, August and February.
Mark Twain

1 | What are shares?

Businesses need capital to get started, and even more to expand and grow. They can raise this from the pockets of managers or their families, as well as from banks and venture capitalists, but at some stage they need more than such sources have available. In addition, there comes a time when some of the original investors want to cash in their profits by selling their holdings.

One popular way of raising money was invented by the Dutch right at the start of the 17th century. It gives backers a receipt that shows that in return for their funding they own part of the company, that they have a share of the business (hence the name). They are not lenders, they are the owners. If there are 100,000 shares on issue, someone having 10,000 of them owns a tenth of the business. That means the chairman and managing director and the rest of the board are the shareholders' employees just as much as the shop-floor foreman or the tea lady. Being a shareholder carries all sorts of privileges, including the right to appoint the board and the auditors (see Chapter 22).

In return for risking their money, shareholders of successful companies get a portion of the profits in the form of dividends. The problem for the investor is getting his or her original capital back. It is hard to find anyone prepared to buy the shares and even if someone is found, setting a fair price is going to be a struggle. That is why companies 'go public'.

QUOTED SHARES

Once a company gets its shares quoted on the stock exchange there is a continuously updated, generally known, market price that is usually far higher than the one at which the original investors put their money into the fledgling business. In addition, there is a 'liquid' market, meaning there are large numbers of potential or actual traders in the paper and so holders of the shares have a far greater chance of finding buyers, and people who want to put money into the business have ready access.

Unlike debentures or gilts there is no redemption date for ordinary shares, though some companies do occasionally buy them back if the price gets low or they want to improve the apparent earnings per share. So in the main the only way for a shareholder to recover the investment is to sell on the stock market.

Blue chips

Despite the frequent reassurance from all the professionals that getting involved in the stock market is a safe way of investing one's money with prolonged long-term growth, there are occasional hints that all is not as it seems. It is not those little notices at the bottom of advertisements and documents required by legislation to warn us that shares can go down as well as up – that will come as no surprise to anyone with enough brains to tie their own shoelaces. It is a clue that the whole confident, pinstriped, smooth and reassuring air of a careful business proposition hides an element of gambling. The major difference is that the only way to win at true gambling is to own the casino or to be a bookmaker, while in the world of the stock market the chances of a total loss are relatively small and with careful investment the prospects are pretty good.

'It is usually agreed that casinos should, in the public interest, be inaccessible and expensive. And perhaps the same is true of Stock Exchanges', wrote John Maynard Keynes in 1935. He himself made a small fortune on the exchange, but it is salutary to be reminded from time to time of the analogy and the comparable risks. The term 'blue chip' is an example. The highest value of gambling chips in poker was traditionally blue, so by analogy the stocks with the highest prestige were reckoned to be similar. So the companies described as being blue chip are the largest, safest businesses on the stock market.

The companies in the FTSE 100 Index, being the hundred biggest companies in the country by stock market valuation, are by definition all blue chips. That is reckoned to make them the safest bets around. The theory is not unreasonable – large companies are more stable than small ones; they can hire the best managers and fund the biggest research budget; they have the financial muscle to fight competition; their very size attracts customers; and the large issued share capital provides a liquid equity market with many small investors and so maintains a steadier price.

The corollary is that the share price movements should be less violent, giving stability and fewer chances for hopping in and out, and the yield and dividend growth are likely to be less than on some riskier investments. So blue chip shares are, in the traditional phrase, 'the investment for widows and orphans'.

However, there is a caveat. Blue chips are safer than a company set up last year by a couple of undergraduates with a brilliant idea, but they are never completely safe. They may be about the most solid there is but they still need to be watched. As an illustration, it is instructive to look back at the Index of the largest companies of even 25 years ago and see how few remain. Remember that companies like British Leyland, Rolls-Royce and Polly Peck were all in the Index at one time, and all went bust. And even the ones that do not completely collapse can fall out of favour or have shoddy managers and so shrink to relative insignificance.

All this applies even to the multinational darlings that were reckoned deep blue. Just consider the fate of the major American airlines of the past 20 years or the way established giants have been rocked by technological changes – in the world of computers IBM and Apple are obvious examples.

That is why tracker funds have been set up. They buy most of the Index shares (ie all the blue chips) and so follow its totality rather than being lumbered with a few of the members and thus being vulnerable to the upsets of one or two of them. Buying blue chips reduces the chances of a disaster, mitigates the chances of great capital growth and should ensure a steady dividend flow, but there are no guarantees. You will almost certainly do better than putting your money anywhere else, but remember that even if you play with the highest chips you can still lose at poker.

RETURNS

Shareholders benefit twice over: they get dividends as their part of the company's profits, and because the business is doing well the value of the shares goes up, so when they sell they get capital appreciation as well. The return on shares over the long term has been substantially better than inflation or the growth in pay and substantially better than most other homes for savings (see Chapter 6).

There is also a degree of protection if things go badly. If the company fails to make a profit shareholders get nothing, and if it goes bust they are at the back of the queue for getting paid. On the other hand, one of the reasons a business is incorporated (rather then being a partnership, say) is that the owners, the shareholders, cannot lose more money than they used to buy the shares. That is in sharp contrast to a partnership where each partner has unlimited personal liability – they are liable to the debts of the business right down to their last cuff-links, or to their last earrings. So even if an incorporated company goes spectacularly broke owing millions of pounds, the creditors cannot come knocking on the shareholders' doors.

STOCK MARKETS

The language of investment sometimes seems carefully designed to confuse the novice. For instance, shares are traded on the stock exchange not the share exchange. Nobody really knows why it came to be called the stock exchange. One theory has it that it was on the site of a meat and fish market in the City and the block on which those traders cut are called stocks. An alternative theory has it that stocks of the pillory kind used to stand on the site. In the Middle Ages the receipt for tax paid was a tally stick with appropriate notches. It was split in half, with the taxpayer getting the stock and the Exchequer getting the foil or counterstock. Some have suggested the money from investors was used to buy stocks for the business, or that stocks were generalized to be a store of value.

When the Greshams picked up a good Dutch idea and built the Royal Exchange as a trading venue, they were forbidden by Elizabeth I from calling it a _bourse,_ as that was a nasty foreign word, and indeed is still the name for the Paris stock exchange just as _börse_ is the name of the Frankfurt exchange.

There are other problems with the language of investments. Shares are what companies issue to shareholders though they are sometimes also called equities. Either way, it seems puzzling to have them dealt in at the stock exchange. Strictly speaking, in the purists' definition, stocks are really bonds – paper issued with a fixed rate of interest, as opposed to the dividends on shares which vary with the fortunes of the business. However, in loose conversation 'stocks' are sometimes used as a synonym for 'shares'. Just to confuse things further, Americans call 'ordinary shares', 'common stock'.

2 | Are there other types of paper?

The ingenuity of City financiers has produced a wide variety of paper issued by businesses. In addition to ordinary shares and various types of bonds there are convertibles, preference shares, deferred, and so on, plus combinations of those categories.

Shareholders are owners of a business who put up the cash to run the company, but it may need additional finance and some of that can come from borrowing. A part of the borrowing may be just a bank overdraft, but to pay for long-term investments most managers reckon it is wiser to borrow long term. For some of this the business issues a different type of paper – in effect a corporate IOU. The generic name for these is bonds: they are tradable, long-term debt issues with an undertaking to pay regular interest (normally at a rate fixed at the time of issue) and generally with a specified redemption date when the issuer will buy it back. Some have extra security by being backed by some corporate assets and some are straight unsecured borrowings. In fact gilts (see Chapter 3) are also a type of bond.

Here as elsewhere in the book you had better get used to words like 'generally', 'usually', 'often', 'normally' and suchlike. This is not a cover for ignorance or lack of research but merely an acceptance of the City's ingenuity. Variants of ancient practices are constantly being invented, and novel and clever financial instruments created to meet individual needs. What is described is the norm, but investors should be prepared for occasional eccentricities or variants.

LOAN STOCK AND DEBENTURES

The bonds that have no specified security to back up the guarantee of regular interest payments are called loan stocks or notes. These offset the greater risk by paying a higher rate of interest than debentures that are secured against assets. Both types of issue differ from shares in many ways – for instance the paper representing debts must receive interest whether the company is making a profit or not. In Britain debentures are usually secured against a fixed asset, but in the United States there is often a floating charge secured on corporate assets in general.

Interest payments on these bonds (called dividends, like the return on shares) come regularly irrespective of the state of the company's fortunes. As the rate of interest is fixed, the market price of the paper will go up when interest rates are coming down and vice versa to ensure the yield from investing in the paper is in line with the returns obtainable elsewhere in the money market. In other words the investment return on the bonds at any particular moment is governed more by the prevailing interest rates than by the state of the business issuing them. The further off the maturity date the greater the volatility in response to interest rate changes because they are less dominated by the prospect of redemption receipts. On the other hand, the oscillations are probably much less spectacular than for equities, where the price is governed by a much wider range of economic factors not just in the economy but also in the sector and the company.

Because the return is fixed at issue, once you have bought bonds you know exactly how much the revenue will be, assuming the company stays solvent and the security is sound, right up to the point of redemption when the original capital is repaid. Since there is still that lingering worry about whether any specific company will survive, the return (generally referred to as the coupon) is a touch higher than on gilts (see Chapter 3), which are reckoned to be totally safe. So for a private investor this represents a pretty easy decision: how confident am I that this corporation will survive long enough to go on paying the interest on the bonds, and is any lingering doubt offset by the return being higher than from gilts?

If the issuer defaults on the guaranteed interest payments – which is generally only when the business goes belly-up – debenture holders can appoint their own receiver to realize the assets, which act as their security and so repay them the capital. Unsecured loan stockholders have no such option but still rank ahead of shareholders in the share-out when the company goes bust.

There are variants on the theme. A subordinated debenture, as the name implies, comes lower down the pecking order and will be paid at liquidation only after the unsubordinated debenture. Most of the bonds, especially the ones issued by American companies, are rated by Moody's and by Standard & Poor's with a graded system from AAA for comfortingly safe down to D for bonds already in default.

There are a few index-linked corporate bonds, but for a private investor gilts are probably a better bet.

WARRANTS

Warrants are a form of security that are often issued alongside a loan stock, and give the owner the right to buy ordinary shares normally over a specified period at a predetermined price, known as the exercise or strike price. They are also issued by some investment trusts. Since the paper therefore has some easily definable value, warrants are traded on the stock market, with the price related to the underlying shares: the value is the market price of the share minus the strike price.

They can gear up an investment. For instance, if the share stands at 100p and the cost of converting the warrants into ordinary shares has been set at 80p, the sensible price for the warrant would be 20p. If the share price now rises to 200p, the right price for the warrant would be 120p (deducting the cost of 80p for converting to shares). As a result, when the share price doubled the warrant price jumped six-fold.

This type of issue is in a way more suited for discussion under the heading of derivatives, like futures and options (see Chapter 4).

PREFERENCE SHARES

Preference shares can be considered a sort of hybrid. They give holders similar rights over a company's affairs as ordinary shares (equities), but commonly holders do not have a vote at meetings; like bonds they get specified payments at predetermined dates. The name indicates their privileged status, since holders are entitled to a dividend whether there is a profit or not, which makes them attractive to investors who want an income, and for some there is a tax benefit to getting a dividend rather than an interest payment. No dividend is allowed to be paid on ordinary shares until the preference holders have had their bit. They rank behind debenture holders and creditors for payouts at both liquidation and dividends. If the company is so hard up it cannot afford to pay even the preference dividend, the entitlement is 'rolled up' and paid in full when the good times return for issues with cumulative rights. Holders of preference shares without the cumulative entitlement usually have rights to impose significant restrictions on the company if they do not get their money. Sometimes when no dividend has been paid the holders get some voting rights.

Like ordinary shares they are generally irredeemable, so there is no guaranteed exit. If the company folds, holders of preference shares rank behind holders of debt but ahead of the owners of ordinary shares.

There are combinations of various classes of paper, so for instance it is not unknown for preference shares also to have conversion rights attached, which means they can be changed into ordinary shares.

CONVERTIBLES

Some preference shares and some corporate bonds are convertible. This means that during their specified lives the holders receive a regular dividend income but there is also a fixed date when the issues can be transformed into ordinary shares – conversion is always at the owner's choice and cannot be forced by the issuer.

Being bonds or preference shares with an embedded call option (see Chapter 4), the value is a mixture of the share price and hence the cost of conversion, and the income they generate.

3 | What are gilts?

The term is an abbreviated version of 'gilt-edged securities'. The suggestion is that of class, distinction and dependability. The implication is that these bonds, issued by the British government, are safe and reliable. There is some justification for this claim: the government started borrowing from the City of London in the 16th century, and it has never defaulted on either the interest or the principal repayments of any of its bonds. Although gilts are a form of loan stock not specifically backed by any asset, the country as a whole is assumed to stand behind the issue and therefore default on future gilts is pretty unlikely as well – the risk is reckoned to be effectively zero.

The securities exist because politicians mortgage the future of the country. When they think tax revenues are suffering only because the economy is in a brief dip and want to bridge that short-term deficit, or they dare not court voter disapproval by raising taxes to cover state expenditure, the difference is made up by borrowing – this is the Public Sector Borrowing Requirement, much discussed by politicians and the financial press. Governments borrow by issuing a sort of loan stock with a fixed rate of interest and a specified redemption date (usually a range of dates to give the government a bit of flexibility) when the Treasury will buy back the paper. Some are called Treasury stock and some have other names, but these have no relevance to anything and are merely to distinguish one issue from another.

The interest rate set on issue (also called the coupon) is determined by both the prevailing interest rates at the time, and who the specific issue is aimed at. The vast majority of the gilts on issue are of this type. In addition there are some index-linked gilts and a couple of irredeemables including the notorious War Loan – people who backed the national effort during World War Two found the value of their savings eroded to negligible levels by inflation – but although this is still an issue it is significant only for economic historians.

There is a long list of gilts being traded with various dates of redemption. For common use these are grouped under shorts, which have lives of under 5 years, medium-dated with between 5 and 15 years to go, and longs with over 15 years to redemption. They are in three such tables in the newspaper prices pages as well. In those tables there are two columns under 'yield'. One is the so-called running yield, which is the return you would get at that quoted price (for an explanation of yields calculations see Chapter 12), and the other is the redemption yield, which calculates not just the stream of interest payments but also the value of holding them to redemption and getting them repaid – always at £100 par (the face value of a security). That is why the two differ. If the current price of the gilt is below par the redemption yield is higher than the running yield, but if the price is above par (which generally suggests it is a high-interest stock) one will lose some value on redemption, so the return is lower.

Since the return is fixed at issue, when the price of gilts goes up, the yield goes down. So if you buy a gilt with a nominal face value of 100p (yes, that is £1 but the stock market generally prefers to think in pence), and with an interest rate set at issue at 10 per cent, but the current price of that issue is 120p, you would get a yield of 8.3 per cent (10p as a percentage of the 120p paid). If the price of that issue then tumbles to 80p you could get a yield of 12½ per cent (10p as a percentage of 80p).

In addition there are other public bonds of only slightly higher risk than gilts. Theses include bonds issued by local authorities and overseas governments. It is not hard to assess the risk of these. How likely is it that a UK local authority will renege on a bond or become insolvent? How plausible is it that French or German states will be unable to pay their debts in the foreseeable future? Admittedly, one can make mistakes in this, as any collector of unredeemed bonds will testify. Chinese governments, czarist Russia, American states, Latin American enterprises and so on have all issued beautifully engraved elaborate bonds that are now used to make lampshades or framed decorations for the lavatory because they were never redeemed.

To compensate for this slightly higher risk, local authority and foreign government bonds have a slightly higher yield, and corporate bonds sometimes slightly higher still, depending on the issuer and guarantor (often a big bank). The differences are generally marginal for the major issuers, seldom much more than 0.3 per cent. In theory, bondholders rank above the holders of ordinary shares if the issuer goes under, but in practice this seldom yields much in the way of repayment.

4 | What are derivatives?

The derivatives market trades in things that depend on or derive from an underlying security, which also determines the price of the derived investment. In other words, these are financial products derived from other financial products. The term is usually taken to cover futures, options and swaps, but there is a growing menagerie of ever more exotic and complex instruments.

This is a highly geared way of betting on the future and is an area for the more experienced and knowledgeable investor. The original purpose of inventing most of them was to reduce somebody's risk – a sort of hedging device. It works in commodities, for instance, when a farmer tries to protect himself from the potential hazard of a huge harvest (of wheat, oranges, coffee and so on) with the consequent plummeting prices, by agreeing a price earlier and before the size of the harvest is known. If the crop turns out to have been meagre he has forfeited the huge profit from a big price hike, but saved himself from penury if it had gone the other way.

FUTURES

Futures contracts in the financial markets followed the ones for commodities and are also used by companies and investors to protect themselves. The facility, as with so many derivatives, was originally created as a way of 'hedging' or offloading risk. For instance, a business exporting to the United States can shield itself against currency fluctuations by buying 'forward' currency. That provides the right to have dollars at a specific date and at a known exchange rate, so it can predict the revenue from its overseas contract. If some shares had to be sold at some known date

Does your current portfolio require a little more flexibility?

Spread Betting with City Index

...ditionally, trading stocks and indices can be difficult and ...exible. With City Index you can take a long or short ...sition on numerous UK, US and European stocks, indices ...d commodities. Our real time trading platform provides ...u with the flexibility needed to trade in today's moving ...rkets. Combined with a host of trading tools, the City ...dex package is invaluable.

...y Index also provide a stop loss facility on certain markets, ...ing clients the ability to limit their losses. Margined ...ding is another feature which allows City Index clients to ...de with a typical initial deposit of 10% of the total ...ntract value.

...y Index do not charge commission, stamp duty or ...kerage, and with our tight spreads, extended trading ...urs and the possibility of tax free profits*, trading with ...y Index could provide the flexibility your portfolio ...quires.

... key feature of spread betting is the leverage that it ...ords. Fluctuations in the value of the underlying ...trument can quickly lead to profits or losses which can ...ceed the initial deposit. Ensure you fully understand the ...ks, as spread betting is not suitable for everyone.

The benefits

- All profits free of UK Capital Gains Tax*
- No commission, brokerage or stamp duty
- Ability to bet on markets going down as well as up
- Extended trading hours on certain markets
- No foreign exchange costs - bet on foreign equities in Sterling
- Margined Trading
- Fully interactive online dealing
- Guaranteed stop losses on certain markets

CITYINDEX
www.cityindex.co.uk

To request a brochure or open an account call
020 7550 8599

Authorised and Regulated by The Financial Services Authority
*Spread Betting profits and losses are not currently subject to
UK Capital Gains tax. Tax laws may change.

Ref: Telegraph book

City Index was established in 1983 and consisted of a couple of dealers, a compliance officer and a coffee lady bringing the under worked staff lunch and refreshments. In the 20 years that passed the company has gone through a couple of market crashes, a recession, a staggering bull market and an ensuing bear market only matched by the one in the 1930s.

Throughout the turbulent years our client base has grown from a handful of city traders to an army of more than 10,000 traders and speculators from all walks of life.

Spreadbetting became the entry point to the financial markets for those who had been put off by exorbitant commissions and fees charged by the stockbrokers around the country. City Index was the answer.

City Index has become a hypermarket of the financial world, a one-stop for financial instruments. So whether you trade individual stocks in the FTSE 100 index, or currencies like the Euro or Sterling against the US Dollar, it is taking place under the same roof. You can trade all the major European and American stocks and indices. You can trade, bonds, and commodities such as gold and wheat. You can even trade pork bellies.

Our aim is to give our clients what they want: fast access to the world's financial markets, but most importantly we offer lightning fast execution. Our professional trading platform is unique in the industry. We operate a principle we call "what you see is what you get." In essence this means that the price you see on the screen will be the price you will deal at.

Spread betting on financial markets with City Index is a flexible and tax-efficient alternative to using traditional futures and/or stockbrokers. It enables the client to bet in the financial futures markets for speculative purposes or for hedging existing portfolios or liabilities.

The two most significant advantages of spread betting on financial markets are that it is currently free of Capital Gains tax and that you can bet on margin. Other advantages include instant execution and the ability to bet with large and small sizes.

These attractive advantages among others have made spread betting the most talked about financial service of recent times, and City Index is proud to be one the leading firms offering this exciting proposition.

The newest product to arrive in the superstore is CFDs, or Contracts for Difference. While spread betting gives a spread around the current market price, the CFD is trading at exactly as the market price. CFDs are now being used as an investment vehicle by retail investors. CFDs are ideal for short term technical trading as well as for hedging positions in the underlying market. Whilst giving the investor all the benefits of the underlying equity market, they enable an investor to avoid many of the costs and problems involved in the purchasing of physical shares. Now City Index offers retail clients the opportunity to trade on the same terms as many large institutions.

(say to satisfy a debt) and an investor was nervous that the market might shift against him in the meantime, it is possible to agree a selling price now.

Simply stated, a futures contract binds two sides to a later transaction. It is an obligation to buy or sell an agreed quantity of an investment or other financial product (anything from shares through gilts to currency – and there are also commodities futures) at a specified future date. For example, the gambler decides to buy a futures contract of £1,000 (it almost does not matter what lies behind the derivative – it could be grain, shares, currencies, gilts or chromium). It costs only 10 per cent margin, in this case £100. Three months later the price is up to £1,500, so the lucky person can sell at a £500 profit which is five times the original stake. It could also happen though that the price drops to £500 and he or she decides to get out before it gets worse. On the same reckoning the loss of £500 is also five times the original money. This shows that unlike an investment in shares or warrants where the maximum loss is the amount of the purchase money, the possible downside of a futures deal is many times the original investment.

Futures contracts can be sold before the maturity date and the price will depend on the price of the underlying security. If you fail to act in time and sell a contract, there could be a pile of pork bellies or manganese or whatever delivered to your front garden.

There is also an 'index future', which is an outright bet similar to backing a horse, with the money being won or lost depending on the level of the index at the time the bet matures. A FTSE 100 Index future values a one-point difference between the bet and the index at £25.

An extension of this is 'spread trading'. The spread betting company, say, quotes a company's shares at 361 to 371p. If you think the shares will rise by more than that you 'buy' at 371p in units of £10. If you are right and the price then goes to 390p, the shares have appreciated by 19p above your betting price (assuming one unit) and the proceeds are therefore £190. That sounds good until you consider that if the shares had instead dropped to 340p, your losses would be £210. Conversely, if you think the shares will fall by more than the quoted spread, you 'sell' at 361p and the same mathematics applies the other way. If the price remains within the 361 to 371p range nobody wins.

Only a small amount of money (the so-called margin) is paid at the time the contract is made, so the potential profit margin is geared up enormously. Helped by the absence of capital gains tax on the proceeds, this is the fastest-growing activity on the stock market. However, the steep downside has lost some people huge amounts, which prompted the Financial Ombudsman and the Financial Services Authority to issue a public warning about the risks.

This is not the acquisition of assets as an investment, but a gamble, and is more suitable for people with expertise and the time to watch movements than for novices or amateurs.

FORWARD CONTRACTS

A futures contract is an agreement. It is about commodities, currencies or financial instruments, but the point is the two sides agree to do a deal at some time in the future. By contrast, a forward contract is a deal there and then, but for future delivery. The contract is at the 'spot' price (currently prevailing) with a specified date for completion when the goods arrive. It is a less common transaction in financial instruments.

OPTIONS

These provide merely the right to sell or buy something as opposed to the obligation incurred by a futures contract. So buying a 'put' option conveys the right to sell a set parcel of shares (normally 1,000) at a specified price at an agreed time (say three months hence). If during that time the share price has fallen significantly, the investor can make a handsome profit by buying the cheaper shares and selling them at the agreed price. Similarly in reverse, a 'call' option conveys the right to buy shares, which is handy if you think they will rise substantially in the interim. Come the contracted day, however, and the price has moved the wrong way, one can just walk away and choose not to exercise the option. All that has been lost is the margin of option money, which is a lot less painful than if the underlying security had been bought and sold.

Like most such 'derivatives', the options can be traded before maturity. This is another way of hedging one's position. Say somebody knows that for some reason he or she will have to sell a parcel of shares in eight months time – to fund the down payment on a house for instance. If there is a worry that the market may slump in the meantime, this provides a way of buying protection: buying a 'put' option at roughly today's price. If it is one of the 70 or so companies with options traded in the market, there is also the chance to sell the option before expiry.

A company languishing in a troubled sector may look to an astute observer to be about to turn itself round, become a recovery stock, and astonish everyone. But if the observer is also astute enough to have misgivings about such uniquely prescient insight, and worries about committing too much money to the hunch, there is a cheap way in. One simply buys an option to buy.

So if Bathplug & Harbottle shares are standing at 75p, it can cost say 6p to establish the right to buy shares at that price at any time over the next three months. If in that time the shares do in fact fulfil the forecast and jump to 120p, the astute investor can buy and immediately sell them at a profit of 39p a share. If the misgivings prove justified and the shares fail to respond or even slump further, only 6p instead of 75p has been lost.

The whole thing works the other way as well. The suspicion but not total certainty that a company is about to be seriously hammered by the market could prompt someone to buy a put option – the right to sell the shares at a specified price, within an agreed set of dates.

These rights have a value as well, related to how the underlying share is performing and how long they have to run, so they can be traded, mostly on the London International Financial Futures and Options Exchange (generally abbreviated to Liffe but pronounced 'life' rather than like the river flowing through Dublin). The traded options market deals in parcels of options for 1,000 shares and at several expiry dates, with some above and some below the prevailing market price for about 70 of the largest companies.

COVERED WARRANTS

Relatively new to Britain is the covered warrant, which in essence is a more flexible option that is easier to deal in and has a much wider range of choices. Germany launched its version in 1989 and it is so popular the country cannot get a lottery going to compete with it. In 2003 the European market – the Swiss and Italians have a version as well – was worth £30 billion.

A covered warrant is the right to buy or sell an asset at a fixed price (called the exercise price) up to a specified date (called the expiry date, anything from three months to five years at issue). The warrant can be based on an individual share but it can also be based on a wide variety of other financial instruments such as an index like the FTSE 100, a basket of shares (including the Questor column choices of shares in the _Daily Telegraph_) or a commodity such as gold, silver, currency, oil, or even the UK housing market.

As with other derivatives, investors can use it to gear up their speculation, as a way of hedging against a market change or even for tax planning. Unlike corporate warrants, which are issued by a company to raise money, a covered warrant is issued by a bank or other financial institution as a pure trading instrument. Covered warrants can be either American (exercised any time before expiry) or European (exercised only on date specified) but most are simply bought and then sold back to the issuer before expiry. If a warrant is held to expiry, it is automatically bought back for cash with the issuer paying the difference between the exercise price and the price of the underlying security.

There are four issuers offering over 500 warrants and certificates on single shares and indices in the UK and around the world. They tend to be major global investment banks which have 'bid' (buy) and 'offer' (sell) prices for their warrants during normal market hours in exactly the same way as shares. Investors trade in them through a stockbroker, bank or financial adviser, just as with ordinary shares. Launched in 2002, there are now more than 70 brokers trading.

A covered warrant costs less than the underlying security; this provides an element of 'gearing', so when the price of the under-lying moves, the price of the warrant moves proportionately further. It is therefore riskier than buying the underlying asset. So a relatively small outlay can produce a large economic exposure which makes warrants volatile, and that means they can produce a large return or lose the complete cost of the warrant price (confusingly called the premium) if the underlying security falls below the purchase price (it is 'out of the money'). In addition, warrants have limited lives and their value tends to erode as the expiry date approaches.

Covered warrants can be used to make both upwards and downwards bets on an underlying asset. Buying a 'call' is a bet on an upward movement. Buying a 'put' is a bet on a downward movement. With both kinds of bet the most an investor can lose is the cost of the warrant. Covered warrants are like options but are freely traded and listed on a stock exchange – they are securitized. As a result, they are unlike options in that they are easy to buy and sell for ordinary private investors through the usual stockbroker.

5 | What about overseas shares?

A substantial number of foreign companies are quoted on the London Stock Exchange, especially from Europe (eg Volkswagen, Bank of Ireland, Bayer, St Gobain, Thyssen Krupp, Ericsson), the United States (Ford), Canada (Seagram), Australia, Japan (Dai Ichi Kangyo, Mitsubishi) and South Africa (South African Breweries). Most of them also trade in Britain, so it is possible to get some idea of the business and some stockbroker analysis on the management and figures, making trading in these pretty well like investing in a major UK company.

The merger of European stock markets makes it easier to get access to these and their shares, especially as there are a large number of rather good Internet-based stockbrokers based in Germany, France and Holland (see Useful addresses, at the back of this book).

It is theoretically possible to buy overseas shares through a UK broker – though in practice not many of them offer the service – and even easier over the Internet with some online brokers. But despite the growth of European traders most of the readily available trade in overseas shares is for US stocks. That looks set to change as an ever-growing number of cut-price dealers from Germany and France set up Net services in Britain.

As with all such investments a degree of research and homework is essential (see Chapter 13). The trouble is that in overseas shares there are added levels of risk. The first is the state of the overseas economy. An investor needs to know whether interest rates are on the verge of change in that country, because that might have an immediate effect on share prices, or whether the economy as a whole is about to soar away or is heading for a precipice.

Then a wise investor gets to know something about the state of a particular sector, so one needs to know whether it is about to be affected by a trade agreement, a reorganization, a spate of mergers and so on. Finally, it is a little harder to keep track of the companies – British newspapers tend not to write about them, stockbrokers do not analyse their figures and one cannot keep an eye on their products and services in the marketplace. There are also local peculiarities; for instance Swiss shares, which are commonly £5,000 each and can go to over £20,000 for a single share. That makes it harder for a small investor to get a range of these stocks – though to be fair there are ways of buying part of a share.

On top of that there is the exchange risk: a comfortable profit from trading in the shares might be completely wiped out by the relative movement of sterling. Finally, there are risks in the way the market itself operates. Regulation in major countries like Australia and the United States is comparable with Britain, but 'emerging' markets can range from the haphazard to the corrupt. As part of that there may also be erratic recording of deals, ownership records may be variable, and controls wayward.

There are people who can cope with all those dangers and have done very well from US shares, and even from investing in the budding markets of smaller countries. Mostly they know what they are getting into and know something of the circumstances to manage the risk.

For a novice to the stock markets or someone with a relatively small amount of money to play with, it is probably wiser to buy investment or unit trusts with the sort of overseas profile you fancy (see Chapter 6). There is a great variety on offer: you can decide whether to opt for Japan, the United States or Germany; for Pacific Rim, Western Europe, or developing countries; and even whether to pick specific industrial sectors within these regions. That not only hands over to professionals the decision on which are the good shares, but also spreads the risk. Another choice is to buy the shares of a UK company that does a lot of trade in the favoured area; this eliminates the foreign exchange consideration since the dealings are in sterling.

6 | How do shares compare with investment/unit trusts?

The main benefits of pooled investments such as unit or investment trusts is the reduction of risk: you get a spread of investments over a number of companies, which cuts the danger of any one of the companies performing badly or going under. Another advantage is administration by a market professional.

INVESTMENT TRUSTS

Investment trusts are pretty straightforward: they are companies like any other, but their only function is to invest in other companies.

They are called closed-end funds because the number of shares on issue is fixed and does not fluctuate no matter how popular or disdained the fund might be.

This sort of vehicle is a convenient means for a small investor without enough spare cash to buy dozens of shares as a way of reducing the risk of any one of them doing badly or even going bust.

A trust will have its money spread across dozens, possibly hundreds, of companies, so a problem with one can be compensated by a boom at another. In addition, the investment managers are professionals, so in theory they will do better than the average layman.

In practice they turn out to be human and fallible. The good ones stand out as being consistently better performers and able to sniff out the changes in economies and sectors in advance and so outperform the market pretty consistently. Not all are brilliant however; some are pretty humdrum. There are also pressures on them to which the private investor is immune. For instance, there is a continual monitoring of their performance, so there is no chance to allow an investment prospect the time to mature for a number of years before reaching its full potential if that means in the meantime their figures are substantially below those of their rivals. A private investor on the other hand can afford to be patient and take a long-term view.

Similarly, it is a brave manager who decides to stick his or her neck out and take a maverick course that differs from the other funds. There will be praise if the course is right and the sack if it's not. Stick with the same sort of policies as all the others however, and the bonuses will probably keep rolling in for not being notably worse than the industry average.

Most funds have enormous amounts of money to invest and unless they are set up to pursue a specific sort of share – say high-tech start-ups, or companies with a small market capitalization – they are generally driven to buying blue chips. There is nothing wrong in that of course, but it does mean they will miss the sudden leap of a smaller company which doubles in price in a couple of months when success finally arrives.

The cost of the stockbroker is the same as it would be with other dealings (though a regular savings scheme with an investment trust is cheaper), and the government stamp duty and the price spread between buying and selling price remain the same.

There are obviously advantages or they would not still be around, much less in such large numbers.

Getting involved does not have to be a random selection of shares, or handing over all decisions to the managers. The investor can exert a certain amount of control and selection by buying the right investment trust shares. There are trusts specializing in the hairier stock markets like Istanbul, Budapest, Manila and Caracas (called emerging markets); there are some investing in the countries of the Pacific Rim, with some of them concentrating on just Japan; some go for small companies; some gamble on 'recovery' companies (which tend to have a fluctuating success record); some specialize in Europe or the United States; some in an area of technology and so on. Managers of investment trusts tend on the whole to be more adventurous in their investment policies than unit trusts.

Some are split capital trusts. These have a finite life during which one class of share gets all the income, and when it is wound up the other class of share gets the proceeds from selling off the holdings.

The trusts are quoted on the stock exchange, so one can tell day by day how the share price is doing. Uniquely one can compare precisely how they are viewed. It is possible to calculate the value of the assets a trust owns – since these are the shares in other businesses, the prices are generally available, except of course for the ones specializing in private companies. Having got the current value of the underlying assets one can then compare it with the trust's own share price. Quite a few will then be seen to stand at a discount to assets (the value of its holdings per share is greater than the market is offering for the trust's own shares), and some at a premium.

One reason many of them are priced differently than their real value is that the major investing institutions avoid trusts. A huge pension fund or insurance company does not have to subcontract this sort of spreading of investments, nor does it have to buy the managerial expertise – it can get them in-house. This leaves unit trusts mainly to private investors who are steered towards them by their accountants and bank managers.

Fashion changes however, and from time to time the investment trust becomes more popular. Buying into one at a hefty discount can provide a decent return – so long as the discount was not prompted by some more fundamental problem with the trust or its management.

UNIT TRUSTS

Unit trusts have the same advantage of spreading the individual's risk over a large number of companies to reduce the danger of one turning sour, and of having the portfolio managed by a full-time professional. As with investment trusts there are specialist unit trusts investing in a variety of sectors or types of company, so one can pick high income, high capital growth, Pacific Rim, high technology or other specialized areas, just as with investment trusts.

But instead of the units being quoted on the stock market as investment trusts are, investors deal directly with the management company. The paper issued therefore has no secondary market – the investor cannot sell it to anyone other than back to the management company. The market is seen from the managers' viewpoint: it sells units at the 'offer' price and buys them back at the lower 'bid' price, to give it a profit from the spread as well as from the management charge. Many of the prices are also published in the better newspapers (see Chapter 12).

These are called open-ended funds, because they are merely the pooled resources of all the investors. If more people want to get into a unit trust, it simply issues more paper and so grows to accommodate them. Unlike the price of investment trust shares, which is set by market demand and can get grossly out of line with the underlying value, the price of units is set strictly by the value of the shares the trust owns.

TRACKER FUNDS

Legend has it that blindfolded staff at one US business magazine threw darts at the prices pages of the *Wall Street Journal* and found their selection beat every one of the major fund managers. And indeed the task of having to do better than the market average consistently over long periods of time is so daunting that very few can manage it.

Some managers have just given up the unequal struggle of trying to outguess the vagaries of the stock market and called themselves 'tracker funds' ('index funds' in the United States). That means they invest in all the big shares (in practice a large enough selection to be representative) and so move with the main stock market index – in the UK that is usually taken to be the FTSE 100.

This gives even greater comfort to nervous investors worried about falling behind the economy, and the policy provides correspondingly little excitement, so it is highly suitable for people looking for a home for their savings which in the medium term at least is fairly risk free – it is still subject to the vagaries of the market as a whole in the short term but on any reasonable time frame should do pretty well.

OPEN-ENDED INVESTMENT COMPANIES (OEICs)

These are a sort of halfway house between unit and investment trusts. Like investment trusts they are incorporated companies that issue shares. Like unit trusts the number of shares on issue depends on how much money investors want to put into the fund. When they take their money out and sell the shares back, those shares are cancelled. The abbreviation OEIC is pronounced 'oik' by investment professionals.

The companies usually contain a number of funds segmented by specialism. That enables investors to pick the sort of area they prefer and to switch from one fund to another with a minimum of administration and cost.

ADVANTAGES

Everything has a cost. Pooled investments reduce the risk and are safer homes for small investors' savings; conversely they are also less likely to hit the admittedly outside chance of a spectacular performer. An investor owning shares in a single company will probably lose the lot if the business fails and calls in the liquidators. But if one of the investments owned by a unit or investment trust falls over it will hurt little because these financial vehicles spread their cash among so many businesses. By the same token there is none of the boost if the share bought is an absolute humdinger and goes soaring into the stratosphere.

The fact that they are safe does not mean the investor should go blundering in without thought or research. Some investment managers for the unit or investment trusts are not awfully clever and fail to do better than the market as whole – in other words they fail to buy the shares that perform better than average. They can be found from the league tables of performance that some newspapers and magazines reproduce, as can the funds with startlingly better performance than both the market and other trusts.

Those tables have to be used with caution however. The performance statistics look only backwards and one cannot just draw a straight line and expect that level of performance to continue steadily into the future. One trust may have done awfully well, but it may just be the fluke of having been in a sector or area that suddenly became fashionable – retail, Japan, biotechnology, financials, emerging markets, etc. There is also the factor that somebody good at dealing with the financial circumstances of 10 years ago may not be as good at analysing the markets of today, much less of tomorrow. On top of that, the chances are that whoever was in charge 10 years ago to take the fund to the top of the league tables will have been poached by a rival company.

The converse holds equally true. A fund may have been handicapped by being committed to investment in Japan, and in the recent period Japan fell out of fashion, or in Internet stocks when the Net lost its glister. Such factors, whether prompted by economic circumstance or fashion, may reverse just as quickly and have the fund at the top of the table. It may also have had a clumsy investment manager who has since been replaced by a star recruited from the competition.

As a vehicle for regular investments, or as an additional safeguard against fluctuating markets, many of these organizations have regular savings arrangements. The investor puts in a regular amount and the size of the holding bought depends on the prevailing price at the time. This is another version of what professionals call 'pound cost averaging'. It also tends to level the risk of buying all the shares or units when the price is at the top.

The rise of both types of trust shows there is a need for some way for small investors to take part in the growth of the stock market without the work and danger of going it alone. They should realize, however, that there are no free rides. For the safety of avoiding the risk of losing all your investment you sacrifice the potentially superior performance of the unlikely chance of backing a spectacularly successful individual share. The chances are that investment and unit trusts are still likely to beat other investments over the longer term.

Management charges for both types of trust are usually high. One way of getting round this is to get into a US mutual fund, which is much the same thing as a unit trust, but has lower charges. The offsetting cost is the exposure to exchange rate risk.

Finally there is the alternative of setting up your own pooled investment vehicle. Investment clubs, hugely popular in the United States, are growing up around the UK at an impressive rate. A group of people get together to pool their cash for putting into the market. The usual method is to put in a set amount, say £10 a month each, and jointly decide what is the best home for it. This has the advantage of being able to spread investments, to avoid management charges, to have the excitement of direct investment, to provide an excuse for a social occasion, and it enables the work of research to be spread among the members (see Chapter 8).

EXCHANGE TRADED FUNDS

There are other ways of tracking an index: exchange traded funds. These are single shares and are traded in the same way but are in effect representative of a whole index, such as the FTSE 100 or an American one such as the Standard & Poors 500. It is a bit like an investment trust with a holding in every company comprising one of the indices, but there is an unlimited number of shares and the price is directly related to the index. There is a slight deviation from the underlying portfolio price but it is very narrow. That also means they can be used in the same way, including 'selling short', and included in ISAs. For a small investor it has all the comforts of a unit or investment trust (the spreading of investments) plus the reassurance of not outperforming a market. That means you will never do better than an

index but also you will not lose your shirt. Moreover there is no stamp duty in the dealing (because they are Irish-registered companies), although there is a management fee charged by the issuers which is generally under 0.5 per cent.

7 | What is the point of owning shares?

There is only a limited number of homes for savings. There are the accounts at banks and building societies, there is property, there are innumerable categories of art and other collectables, from claret to Dinky cars, and there are pension plans and insurance policies (which are to some extent dependent on the performance of the stock market). Which is best depends on how much notice you can give for wanting your money back, how much risk you are prepared to tolerate (on capital, income and by inflation), and how long you are prepared to leave the money untouched. Most people have a range of commitments and set up separate private pots of cash to meet them: so much for the holiday in six months' time, so much for the children's education, a lump put away safe for emergencies, so much to make sure we can pay the mortgage, that bit for pensions, some for a new car and even just a mad splurge, and so on. All of this means that for most people buying shares comes well down the list.

The money that can be released for shares depends on personal risk/reward calculations. Nobody outside can do them for you because the only sensible way to get the right answer is to weight them. For instance, some people are prepared to bet at odds of 14½ million to one against them, which would normally seem insane, but because the cost of taking part in the National Lottery is only £1 and the winnings can run into millions, lots of people are prepared to take a punt. A sort of reverse calculation of that is needed: what sort of reward would you need for the admitted risks of investing in shares? Doing that calculation is subjective because both sides are also subjective – how you assess risk depends on the timescale, the choice of investments, and the range of holdings; the rewards can be demonstrated now by comparing the return from putting the cash on deposit, into gilts (see Chapter 3), or into equities (another word for shares). Equities are usually several percentage points higher than gilts, which in turn are several points above deposit accounts, but how the real return will fare in the future is only some type of extrapolation.

There are various ways of making a profit, but which is important to any individual will determine which type of share to buy. See Chapter 13 for how to sort out priorities.

For the portions of money on which people are prepared to accept a degree of risk and can wait for the right moment before pulling out, the stock market provides a pretty good destination. That means the money put into shares comes under its own separate heading. It is not cash you will need to realize at short notice or to rely on as a source of income for your old age, say.

The stock market is only for people who can spare the cash, not only in the physical sense that it will cause no serious hardship if lost, but also in the psychological sense that you will not lie awake at night fretting about the performance or get ulcers if the business goes down the pan. That second point may be a good test of whether a person is temperamentally suited to be a dabbler on the stock exchange. If you look on it as an alternative to the 3.30 at Haydock, a flutter at the roulette wheel, or the Lottery, and can shrug off declines or even losses without serious distress, the market may suit.

That is not quite a fair assessment of what is involved, since the chances are the horse you back fails to win and then all your money is gone. When putting money into shares, the chances are pretty good that the company will stay afloat and continue to pay dividends, so there will be some return on your investment. The odds are way ahead of other forms of gambling, and the return is better than other forms of investment, and careful research, monitoring and evaluation can certainly reduce risks on the stock market. But the point is about the temperament that can cope with the unpredictable. If short-term oscillations or even the occasional insolvency of one of your investments is likely to upset you really seriously, then it is best for your peace of mind to find another destination for the money. It applies to all stock market-linked vehicles, but especially if you are buying individual companies' shares.

If introspection shows that sort of hazard with hard-earned cash could cause alarm, it does not mean that the stock market and its unquestioned benefits are closed to you. You can still benefit from the long-term performance of shares by the reduced-risk route of pooled investment vehicles (see Chapter 6). The money is still invested in shares, but the dangers of big losses are lessened by the number of companies in which the funds invest and by professional management, with the corresponding cost of failing to make the occasional spectacular gain by picking an outstanding share.

It is also possible to buy a with-profits insurance policy – that guarantees a minimum payment at the end of the term (say 5 or 25 years) or on death, but in addition there are annual and terminal bonuses that are linked to the company's profits and its success in investing on the stock market. As the insurance companies have shown, this is not without hazards, and not just because the companies have a mixed record as investment managers.

Even if you decide to take the plunge, it is a good idea not to put all the available cash into the market at once. That way, if a really wonderful opportunity comes along, there is still something left to take advantage of it.

There are now about 12 million people owning shares in Britain, though a large portion have just one share in a privatization issue or from the free issues at the demutualization of a building society.

There are two ways of investing in the stock market: long term (probably most suitable for the small investor) and as an active trader.

LONG TERM

As all the newspapers, magazines and books say, over the long term the stock market has produced a better return than almost any alternative. On the other hand, as Lord Keynes pointed out, in the long term we are all dead.

Value of £100 invested at the end of 1945, gross income reinvested		
	Nominal	Real
Equities	£97,023	£4,132
Gilts	£3,296	£140
Cash	£4,165	£177
Value of £100 invested at the end of 1990, gross income reinvested		
	Nominal	Real
Equities	£405	£306
Gilts	£324	£245
Index-Linked Gilts	£242	£182
Treasury Bills	£200	£151
Corporate Bonds	£361	£272

Source: Barclays Capital Gilt Study, 2001

Figure 7.1   Comparing values over time

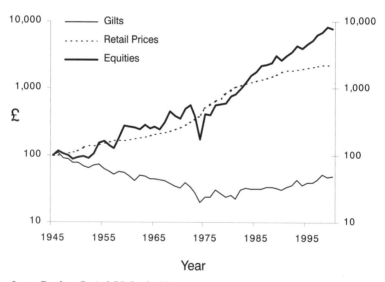

Source: Barclays Capital Gilt Study, 2001

Figure 7.2   Barclays price indices: £100 nominal since 1945

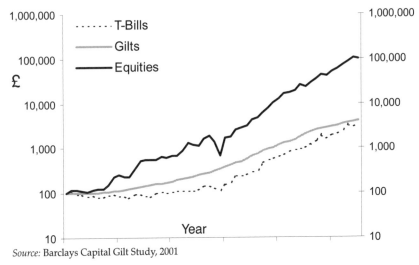

Source: Barclays Capital Gilt Study, 2001

Figure 7.3   Barclays total return indices: nominal terms since 1945

As any chart will show, over a period of 30, 50 or 100 years, returns from shares outperform most other investments. They do better than property, antiques, deposit accounts, fine wines, building society savings, and so on. Since 1918 shares in Britain have on average provided a return of 12.2 per cent a year, compared with say 6.1 per cent produced by the gilt-edged securities issued by governments. Those figures are despite the US market falling 87 per cent between September 1929 and July 1932, the UK index dropping 55 per cent in 1974 and the steep drop following the hurricane in October 1987. There is also the experience of the Far East market, which really took a battering in the 1990s.

Cash in a deposit account would have produced even less than government bonds, probably something under 5½ per cent. Taking a more recent period, from the end of World War Two, equities have on the whole (taking into account both income from dividends and capital appreciation) beaten the inflation rate by 7 per cent or more.

The question is whether this can continue. In effect that is a question about whether our economic system and the process of markets and demand will remain. Many people produce doom-laden scenarios doubting that – anything from global warming causing worldwide floods and weather disruption, through nuclear war, volcanic eruptions causing a new ice age, to super-viruses wiping out millions of people. In most of those cases where you had put your savings is likely to be of marginal significance.

There is the story of the man who, on touching British soil after the Dunkirk evacuation, phoned his stockbroker and bank manager from Folkestone and told them to sell everything he had and put it into shares. 'You must be mad,' they retorted. 'The Germans could invade at any moment and then the companies would be worthless.' 'If they do invade than all bets are off anyway,' he said, 'and it matters little what I owned, but if they do not this will be a winner.' He retired at the age of 45 a wealthy man.

So on average – which is always the important word of warning to bear in mind – shares provide a good long-term home for spare cash. One way to show this is to compare equities with something totally safe and predictable like index-linked gilt-edged securities (see Chapter 3 for a discussion of gilts). The return on shares is almost always higher, and certainly so over the long term. This is to compensate for the greater risk: index-linked gilts are guaranteed, while companies are subject to the vagaries of economic circumstances. The resulting difference – the greater return on equities – is therefore called the 'equity-risk premium'. Just what the correct level of that premium might be is a subject of debate and tends to vary with the perceived risks. On the assumption you will not have to sell the shares to raise cash at any particular moment, you can afford to take the long view over which shares perform best.

There is a tendency to refer to figures that are largely averages. There is a good reason for that. Not only does the stock market as a whole oscillate in the short term – whatever its long-term trend – but individual shares vary from each other and from the market as a whole. One can discuss decades but can say nothing about months. So it is hard to make absolute statements. One can say over the long term that the market as whole has been rising and benefited investors, but that can hide both short-term drops and underperformance by individual shares. That is not a warning to stay away, but merely a reminder that you cannot always rely on the overall or long-term statistics to work in your favour at any specific time. It is because even normally sensible people forget that danger that the government has insisted on the apparently stupid wealth warning on all the literature and advertising that the price of shares can go down as well as up.

Another view is to decide what it is you want from an investment. For instance, another way of looking at shares as an investment is to decide whether you want income or capital growth. These are not absolute alternatives, since any company doing so well that it hands out great dollops of cash in dividends is almost certain to see its share price bound ahead. But not always, as even a cursory glance down the prices page of a newspaper will show the huge disparities in the yield figures. These criteria and ways of assessing the most suitable investments are all discussed in Chapter 13.

Away from equities, there are investment and unit trusts specializing in high-income shares, and gilts provide a safe and predictable income to redemption. In addition, one of the nice things about the stock market is that the income should not be eroded by inflation, but at the very least move with it.

SHORT TERM

There is another way of investing, for the experts and the people prepared to devote time and serious effort to the deal. That is the short-term active trading tactic of taking advantage whenever a share moves sharply enough to make trading worthwhile. You spot a takeover trend, say among food companies, and get in as the other companies start rising; or you detect a growing fashion for a technology – computers, Internet, biotechnology, etc – and pile in as the boom starts to sweep the shares to unrealistic heights. But this also means you have to watch the market like a hawk and see the sell signals in time to get out with a profit.

For people prepared to devote large amounts of time and effort to playing the market, there is the prospect of making a profit from active trading. It demands more spare money because the proportionately higher costs of spreads, brokers' fees and government tax mean you have to deal in larger amounts and achieve bigger share rises to make a profit (see Chapter 9).

One other point – every time one person managed to make a big profit, somebody else missed it. They may not always have made a loss, but just failed to get the real benefit. What makes you think you will be the winner every time, or spot the real successes and avoid the duffers? Some people do have a talent, but not many.

This end of the market, the bouncing in and out by instinct, hunch and being hyper-alert to changes, is the part that takes stock market investment closer to gambling. At the more extreme end is the recent upsurge in 'day trading' (buying and selling within 24 hours), which can be achieved fairly readily over the Internet. The figures from the United States, where the fashion started, suggest that fewer than 5 per cent of the people doing it make money. The moral of which is that some people make a profit, but it is a long way from being an assured way to riches.

PERKS

In addition to the usual benefits of owning shares, such as capital appreciation and dividend income, there are many companies trying to keep shareholders loyal and enthusiastic by providing perks – most of them are merely discounts and therefore entail additional spending by shareholders, which helps profits. For instance, the Channel Tunnel has travel concessions, Barratt Developments gives discounts on buying or renting its properties, Paramount Group gives vouchers worth £20 off meals at its restaurants, and Courts reduces prices of furniture. Companies as various as Iceland, Kwik-Fit, Park Foods and Psion provide benefits. For some there is a minimum holding before the perks kick in.

Hargreaves Lansdown and Premier Fund Managers compile lists of companies with shareholder perks.

8 | How much money does it take?

Most advisers reckon £2,000 is a sensible minimum for a single individual investment. It is possible to deal in smaller amounts at a time, but it puts up an extra barrier to making a return: stockbrokers set a minimum price on transactions and the dealing costs (see Chapter 9) can overwhelm the profit from the transaction. If you are dealing in a small company's shares that have a wide price spread (the difference between the buying and selling price) the threshold for potential profit is raised still further. And there is also a government tax on dealing.

For example, if the dealing cost is £20 for a £500 parcel, the share has to rise by more than 8 per cent just to break even, bearing in mind the likely dealing spread. That means a share standing at 220p would have to rise by over 18p before the investor saw any benefit. It can happen, but it is just stacking the odds against yourself.

Competition among stockbrokers is, however, increasing with the numbers of sites on the Internet rising daily, so the cost could start coming down and with it the minimum economic investment.

Mark Twain said there was nothing wrong with putting all your eggs in one basket, but *watch that basket*. That is unlikely to work for the stock market. Scrutinize a company with all the attention possible, analyse its figures and read all the reports available – and despite all the favourable indications it can still disappear from sight without warning. Sudden external changes can overwhelm sound businesses, and inept managers can so fail to keep track of what is happening under their noses that nobody outside notices either until the liquidator moves in.

the**share**centre:

once a day

once a week

once a month

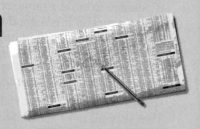

Putting money aside to invest in the stock market every month can be a good habit to get into – it makes it more affordable, and it can help even out the ups and downs of the market too. Open an account with The Share Centre and you'll find we're out to make it easy to do with our regular investment service. Of course, the value of stock market investments can go down as well as up and you may not get back what you originally invested - but we'll give you comprehensive information, interactive tools and free expert advice to help you choose which investments to buy. Visit share.com or give us a call. And get started on making your finances as healthy as you aim to be.

● **www.share.com**
● **0870 400 0204**

For safety therefore one needs to spread the risk over a number of companies. A decent portfolio even for a relatively small investor would contain at least 10 companies. That is the eventual safe haven, however, and it does not of course mean that everyone must start with at least £20,000 going spare or it is not worth even thinking about the stock market – it just means these are the sensible requirements to reduce the much-publicized risks. Just remember that the main aim of investing is to get a decent return for an acceptable risk. With one share the risk is greater, but the more companies' shares you own the less chance there is of your entire stock market holding suddenly collapsing to nothing. So it is possible to build a range of shares over the years. Indeed, most advisers reckon it is a good idea to keep a little float of available cash to take advantage of opportunities.

All these tactics are still variants of the aim of getting a decent return but reducing risks. A really rich investor can put money into property, fine art, venture capital, currency funds, etc, and spread equity investment all round the sectors and the world. That way all risks are hedged. For most of us, offsetting one or two of the dangers is the best we can hope for. The two most obvious ones are that the money will be eroded by inflation, and that all of it will disappear through insolvency.

It is a general rule that the lower the risk, the lower the return – which generates its own obvious warning that if somebody is offering mouth-watering returns or even a profit that seems markedly above comparable destinations for your cash, you may rely on there being a catch. The converse also holds true, however: the higher the risk the higher the potential reward. Invest in a single share and if you strike it lucky the investment can multiply many times in a single year, and for some people with an appetite for danger that offsets the risk that the company could fold and so take every penny of their money with it. This is to dramatize what generally happens – in practice it is far more common for the share you own neither to burst through the roof nor crash through the cellar but to toddle along for months or even years producing little movement in the price.

That £20,000 may look a formidable sum – especially if one thinks about it as the minimum safe level of holding – but set it against a lifetime earnings of over £1 million for even a relatively lowly paid household and it begins to seem a little more do-able. On the other hand, if the total costs listed here and the amount needed to provide a reasonably safe income for your old age seem a touch formidable, there are less daunting alternatives, still with a link to the benefits of the stock exchange, such as investment or unit trusts (see Chapter 6).

INVESTMENT CLUBS

An alternative to pooled vehicles managed by a professional is an investment club. This is just a group of private investors who pool their cash and jointly decide how it should be invested. This has the advantage of spreading holdings over a larger number of investments than any single member could manage, without having to pay the fees of a unit or investment trust or other professional management company. You forfeit the expertise of the unit and investment trust people but have the fun of picking your own shares (though you can opt for any sort of investment) and get a social occasion thrown in as a bonus. The attraction is increasing enormously. In 1997 there were about 350 clubs in the UK, but three years later that had grown to over 7,000 with 60 per cent of the members never having ventured into these waters before.

The ideal number for a club is somewhere between 3 and 20. With more than 20 members the Inland Revenue will call the club a corporation and you will have to start paying corporation tax. Several stockbrokers have packages for investment clubs, such as Barclays, DLJ Direct, Hargreaves Lansdown, NatWest, Charles Schwab, Share Centre and TD Waterhouse.

The specialist charity ProShare publishes a handbook on how to go about starting one and offers some handy advice (see Useful addresses, at the end of this book) and most experts recommend members read other guidance as well to get a broad range of expertise. It is not vital that any member really knows about the intricacies of the stock market, but it is useful to have a range of knowledge among members about, say, engineering, brewing, retailing and so on.

It is vital, however, to get the organization set up on a formal basis or there will be some very painful surprises and arguments later. There are model rules and constitutions available, which everyone has to sign. These set out, among other things, how people may join and leave, a unit valuation system and how decisions are made. In addition, a wide range of other decisions are needed: the level of monthly subscriptions; when and where the members meet; how decisions are made; appointing a chairman, treasurer, and secretary; deciding on bankers, stockbrokers, accountants. You have also to decide whether the club will continue to accumulate a portfolio or whether it is to have a finite life of, say, five years, after which the proceeds are shared out among the members. Some have specified that there be no recriminations if an investment goes wrong. Some formal mechanism has to be set up for the holdings. They can be held by one member (usually the treasurer) on behalf of the rest, or by a nominee company set up for the purpose, or even by a bank.

You might be invited to join an existing club, in which case it is wise to check that all these decisions have already been made and that you feel comfortable with them. Also check that the monthly contribution is in line with what you can afford or would want to put in.

If this route sounds fun, there are still some basic considerations to prevent tears later. First, only get together with people you like and trust, and whose objectives and preferences are similar to your own. If you fancy taking a punt on the latest high-technology start-up or going for risky recovery stocks, it would be a mistake to join a club whose members reckoned buying into Vodafone was pretty racy.

The criteria for choosing investments vary widely among the clubs, but many opt for the riskier end of the market because the club participation is additional to the investments members have already made on their own behalf. So they are generally fairly ready to go for Aim (see Chapter 20), technology stocks and the like. Some even extend beyond the stock market and invest in property directly or indirectly. The main advice of the experts is not to invest in anything you do not understand, and most professionals strongly suggest avoiding the complex and risky end of the market, like derivatives.

Second, it is not a free ride where you can relax on the coat-tails of more expert and hardworking members. Most clubs share out the work and do make it clear that they expect people to participate beyond just putting in the monthly money, even fining them if they turn up late for meetings.

Most clubs invest well under £100 a month – a common figure is about £20 to £40 – so this is not the prerogative of the wealthy. Conversely it is unlikely the proceeds will allow anyone to retire at 30 or to buy a Caribbean island. But you never know – the Hampshire village of Whiteparish has a club that managed a 49 per cent return on its investments (and won the prize for being the best) and even some children's clubs have managed returns pretty close to that. Several have built portfolios worth £500,000. Only a few have done so badly that members have lost their cash.

9 | What does it cost to deal in shares?

More than it should, is the simple answer. As with so many other things, it is more expensive in Britain to trade in shares than in many other industrialized countries. International comparisons have shown cheaper dealing overseas and fewer complaints about speed and information. Some US brokers also allow small investors a chance to get in on the ground floor by participating in a flotation – what they call there an 'initial public offering'. Not that the US brokers themselves are universally regarded as kindly philanthropists. There is a classic book about Wall Street, which has been reprinted regularly over the past 40 years, that comments on the wealth of brokers – it is called, *Where are the Customers' Yachts?* Competition and technology may be changing all that.

For all the loud proclamations by the stock exchange, small individual holders are still considered a nuisance. Small investors deal in small amounts, which cost just as much to transact as large deals, and the shareholders need elaborate protection from sharks and their own folly because otherwise they might sue or generate snide stories in the newspapers, and MPs are likely to kick up a self-interested fuss. However, the market needs the small investor as a counterweight to the unimaginative short-termism of the major institutional holders. Private investors generally also provide a market for smaller companies that are not practical investments for major finance houses.

BROKERS' COMMISSION

The main cost of dealing comes from the broker's commission. That varies depending on the type of broker, the amount of work they are doing and the size of the deal.

Some charge as little as £5 minimum for dealing, but most brokers charge around £12 to £15 minimum per transaction, though there are brokers going as high as £20 to £25, with a commission on a sliding scale above the minimum dependent on the value of the transaction. An order of £2,500 might cost 1½ per cent with the rate falling to ¾ per cent or sometimes even lower on major deals. There may also be a one-off charge of at least £10 for joining Crest, the UK stock exchange's electronic registry of share holdings.

A site on the Internet called www.fool.co.uk provides a guide to charges of Net and telephone brokers. It is not comprehensive and sometimes misses new services or special offers from some of the participants. It is not unusual for a new entrant to buy some market share by enticing in the passing investor through having an introductory period free of charges. A French research company called Blue Sky does its own survey of online brokers throughout Europe and rates their performance at its Web site, but even these tables need further examination because Blue Sky's criteria are likely to differ from those of the average small investor in the UK. Nevertheless this is all added information about what is available.

THE SPREAD

In addition there is the cost of trading. As anyone who has ever tried to sell a second-hand car knows, the price of something is very different depending on whether you are buying or selling. So it is with shares. That is fair enough because the trader needs to eat as well. To make sure he does not starve, this 'spread' varies with the risk. So FTSE 100 companies, like Vodafone, Barclays Bank, British Airways, etc, which have huge market capitalizations, thousands of shareholders and a regular flock of deals every day, would have a relatively narrow spread of say 1 to 1½ per cent; by contrast a tiny company with few shareholders and little trade could have a spread of around 10 per cent.

This incidentally makes those small companies and their shareholders pretty unhappy, because it is a vicious circle. It is twice as hard to make a profit from small-company shares because the shares have to rise even more to make up for the extra gap in the spread. That deters all but the hardiest optimists, which therefore means fewer trades in the shares, so reinforcing the wide spread.

ADVICE

There is lots of free advice from newspapers, magazines, radio, television, newsletters and mailshots (see Chapter 16) but investors still have to collect and sort it all, sift the material and test it to see if any of it is worth acting on. This is not only a long and tedious task but the testing portion is especially dodgy for someone inexperienced in shares. In theory having a professional adviser can improve on that. The stockbroker or adviser can take on board the investor's preferences and needs and so produce tailor-made investment recommendations. Such handholding can be valuable and the good advisers can produce a far better portfolio than an individual who has a living to earn and so cannot spend all day evaluating the options.

There are two points to be made: like everything else worth having it costs money, and no sensible investor hands over the future without asking questions and testing the answers against common sense. Just as an intelligent patient asks the doctor what is wrong and what effects the medicine will have, and a careful client asks the lawyers how the law stands and what the advice is based on, so a shrewd investor should ask financial advisers why they advise such a course and what assumptions lie behind the recommendation. It is at this point that common sense and personal experience re-enter. If you disagree with the adviser's forecasts of the next six months or five years (and your guess is as good as his or hers) it is important to say so, so the portfolio can be adjusted to the satisfaction of both of you.

Such advisers/brokers charge either by commission, or a flat fee, or a commission on trade.

PORTFOLIO MANAGEMENT

Some people get a real buzz from organizing their investments. The combination of gambler's hunch, rational analysis, the prospect of profit, a chance to outsmart the highly paid professionals, and the arcane language of finance is for some people a fascinating pursuit. That is lovely because it creates the best sort of hobby – the sort that makes money.

Without that confidence, enthusiasm and time one can still look after the investments but on a more intermittent basis. People who do this read the City pages of the newspapers and keep up to date with the economic trends; they revalue their investments reasonably regularly and then decide what the best course might be. In the very nature of things, investments for such people tend to be relatively long term.

Another option is to subcontract that work and get professional help with building and managing a portfolio. Though some independent financial advisers and asset management companies will take on portfolios from £25,000 upwards, many of the companies are reluctant to look at you with less than £50,000 to play with – and it would probably not be worth it if they did – and many prefer more than £100,000. This can be done through a formal scheme that brings advice and comment from the stockbroker but still leaves the final decision on buying and selling and the amounts to be put in with the investor.

Another alternative is 'discretionary' management, which passes on the preferences and criteria (see Chapter 13 on how to sort those out) to the broker/manager, who then takes on the job of picking both the stocks and the timing. All this costs money of course – either a flat fee of, say, £1,000 a year, or a percentage of the portfolio managed, which can be ½ to 1 per cent depending on size. It goes without saying that you only hand over this sort of power over your personal finances to someone you trust, but even then keep an eye on them: some stockbrokers have been disciplined for 'churning' – continuously buying and selling to generate commission for themselves.

TAX

After the market-makers, stockbrokers and advisers have taken their fees, the government takes its additional cut from our savings by imposing a tax called stamp duty at the rate of ½ per cent on the value of every deal that has used taxed income. (See also Chapter 27). As the French and German governments do not impose such a tax on their investors and companies, British shareholders can save the tax by trading through those exchanges.

thesharecentre:

we'll get your investing off to a great start.

Interested in investing but don't know how to get going? Start by opening a Share Account with The Share Centre. Use it to buy and sell UK shares, unit trusts and other stock market investments and you'll have access to a wide range of free investment tools to help you along the way. There's market data, news and views about sectors and companies, and free expert advice on hand if you want help steering the right path. So, remembering as always that the value of investments can go down as well as up and you may not get back what you originally invested, click on share.com now or give us a call. And put yourself right in the driving seat.

● **www.share.com**
● **0870 400 0204**

The Share Centre, P.O. Box 2000, Aylesbury, Bucks HP21 8ZB. The Share Centre is a member of the London Stock Exchange and is authorised and regulated by the Financial Services Authority under reference 146768.

10 | Where and how can you buy shares?

Most existing shareholders acquired their holdings in the privatization of nationalized industries, or were simply given a sweetener of some shares to vote in favour of building societies and mutual insurance businesses becoming quoted companies. In addition, more and more people are acquiring a stake in their employer through a variety of share schemes. One consequence is that all these shareholders never had to go through the normal procedures of choosing the share and paying a stockbroker to deal for them. If they want to sell those shares or have decided the stock market looks a promising way of providing for their old age and so want to deal in more shares, they have to go through a broker, just as everyone has had to for centuries.

FINDING A STOCKBROKER

That means registering with the broker in advance. Traditionally a friend or relative introduced you to a stockbroker – it was almost like joining a select club. That was one reason most people had not the faintest notion how to find one or how to tell if the firm was any good. The stock exchange authorities gave out lists but there was little to distinguish one firm from another. In addition, for all their protestations most of them did not want to be bothered by people with only a few thousand pounds to invest and with little knowledge or experience of the stock market.

The banks rather belatedly stepped in to provide share-dealing services, and so has a new breed of transaction-only brokers (they just buy and sell but give no advice on investment). Now more information is becoming available, not just about Internet traders, which is the easiest, but about the low-cost brokers through tables published in many of the more serious newspapers. But even so stockbrokers can take some finding and are rather difficult to compare.

Many brokers will want some advance information before taking on a client. A broker may often need reassurance that its customer can pay, by running a credit check before accepting any orders. For all this folderol finding the right broker is probably not as intimidatingly difficult as it seems at first and getting registered with one of the Internet sites is a doddle.

Among the welcome factors corroding the ancient restrictive practices of the stock exchange is the advent of the Internet. It provides choice. So there is not only the traditional stockbroker (usually the subsidiary of a major financial institution such as a high-street bank or building society) but also a number of independent companies, most of which are members of the Association of Private Client Investment Managers and Stockbrokers, which has a free members list (see Useful addresses at the back of this book). Many of them have their own Web site, so, along with the Web-only outfits, there are well over 100 brokers now on the Internet operating out of several countries, including the UK, Ireland and the United States.

There are two main types of broker: the ones who give advice and will even take over management of the portfolio, and the execution-only firms that buy and sell on demand and do no more. The phone-based and online brokers are all of the latter type.

People who reckon to need help and advice, and realize that service also has a cost but think it is worth it, can go to one of the big high-street financial institutions with branches round the country and advertisements all over the place. (For a selection see Useful addresses.) Alternatively they can seek out a good local firm that is experienced in the needs of small investors and can produce performance equal to any of the biggest names in the country. The best way to find these local outfits is by recommendation, casting the net as widely as possible and trying to get some objective assessment of performance. The second-best way is to go to the Association of Private Client Investment Managers and Stockbrokers.

There is the choice of either an advisory (just suggesting investments) or a discretionary service (managing the portfolio). Discretionary service demands a reasonable minimum amount of initial cash or holdings – the lowest is about £10,000 but £50,000 or £100,000 is more common, and the management fee is about ½ to 2 per cent of the size of the portfolio. The investor hands over the portfolio and gives the broker the right to manage as best he or she can, buying and selling as seems right. One gets a regular report of what the investments are and how much they are worth, plus notification of any dealings. Some will include in this service management of bank accounts, pensions and even insurance. In these cases there is normally a long discussion at which priorities and aims are set. Once the broker knows what you are trying to achieve with your money, the advice can be more sensible and helpful.

For the customer who decides when to deal, a problem that has aroused a lot of complaint has been the occasional hitch in contacting the broker. In 1999 one Jersey-based investor with a prices screen contacted his telephone broker and saw the value of his holdings halve while the stockbroker left him hanging on listening to a recoded message telling him all customer service operatives were busy and he would be connected as soon as one was free. So great were his irritation and frustration at watching the continuing plunge of his investments and his inability to sell that he had a fatal heart attack. This is an extreme case but at least the poor chap did manage to get through, even if it was only to a recorded message – some people, especially on the Net, have had problems getting through to the broker at all.

Before picking a broker, therefore, a few questions are in order, such as service quality, and terms and conditions including redress in such cases. Stockbrokers then act for individual investors by executing their orders in the market. The punter telephones the broker with whom he or she has an agreed account and gives the order to buy or sell. Normally, during the conversation the broker will call up the appropriate page on the computer system and tell the investor just what the price is standing at, and if that is agreeable the deal goes ahead.

THE INTERNET

The big growth in the market comes from the Internet. As the Net itself became the latest fashion it attracted both users and suppliers; fashion or not, it has genuine advantages. For a start, investors can put in an order whenever they feel ready and if they have a communicating system can do it from pretty well anywhere. In addition, an enormous range of information is available on the same screen to help with the decision. Finally, it can reduce costs not just because competition does that anyway but also because the broker does not have to maintain large numbers of elegant-suited smooth young people at hideously expensive City premises.

In practice, the online brokers have not seriously undercut the telephone dealers so far, but competition is changing that and it is possible to deal for a flat fee of £10. This is important for people planning to be active investors, nipping in and out of shares and having to offset dealing costs against profits. According to the Paris-based research outfit called Blue Sky, the four best-value online brokers are all German. Some overseas ones require residence in the country to deal, but in general Belgian, Swiss and Luxembourg brokers are prepared to accept any nationality or residence. You may want to invest on other stock exchanges – though the European ones are in the throes of merging. Then you have to decide what other services you are likely to need, and how you want to deal (e-mail or real time). But beware. There is no control and little monitoring of what passes over the Web.

Nothing comes without drawbacks. Without seeing the people, the buildings, the organization and so on, it is hard to get a feel for how reputable or efficient the broker is and so an investor is driven far more to relying on reputation, recommendation and newspaper opinion. Then there is the constant fear that transactions online can be eavesdropped by shady characters who might also use your particulars to deal for their own profit, or hack into your or your broker's computer and tamper with data. Third, there are always dangers of computer failures. Computers seem to have reached about the level of development and reliability of cars in the late 1920s when drivers had to know about magnetos and drive belts and distributors to cope with the continuous breakdowns. This means that just when you need to deal, one of the machines may be having its wick trimmed or its elastic being changed. Fourth, online trading does not generate share certificates. The shares are still registered to the new owner, but it is all computerized and generally the broker will hold the title to them in a 'nominee' account, which is administratively tidy but could mean the investor cannot easily change allegiance to another broker.

Another danger is the seductive world of computing. Sitting at a home screen with access to all that information it is easy to be lulled into thinking that the data are comprehensive and reliable, and also into making a snap decision. It almost feels like a game using Monopoly money, so one is drawn into making investments at the click of a mouse that could wipe out the family's savings.

To join one of the growing band of online stockbrokers, one needs to get into the Web site and follow the instructions for registering. Many of them demand a cash account from which payments can be made, with almost all of them requiring a float of cash deposited with the brokerage. There is interest on this, but generally below what it could earn elsewhere. The signing-on procedure also gets you to set a password to prevent others looking at, much less tampering with, your investments, and explains the minimum level of software capability needed to get into the system.

The more adventurous still, who want to buy a US share, may want to go through a US broker based in the United States. It is liable to be cheaper than UK stockbrokers, and cheaper even than the European offshoots of US brokers. There is a site that compares the performance of several online brokers on costs, speed of service and other benefits including helping small investors to get a subscription at the time of the first listing – it is at www.europeaninvestor.com.

One of the big thrills in the United States is day trading. This requires spotting the small fluctuations and getting in and out of shares within one day. For all the fashions and the hype, and despite the many books explaining how to make a fortune from day trading, it looks as if hardly any private investors have made any money on the system. And many have lost heavily.

With a Wap-enabled mobile telephone all this can be accessed and organized from anywhere, and some brokers are also introducing voice-recognition systems to provide share prices over the telephone.

There are two sorts of dealing online. One is to send an instruction via e-mail to the broker, who then executes it via his trading screen. In theory he can do that in 15 seconds and within 15 minutes a return e-mail can confirm the deal has been done as instructed. The other method is what is called real-time dealing, in which the investor cuts out the middleman and connects directly to the stock market dealing system.

TRADING

Normally when the instruction is given to deal, the broker will transact 'at best' – buy at the lowest available price and sell at the highest. Another option is to set the broker a limit – the maximum at which you are prepared to buy or the minimum price below which you are not prepared to sell. Usually such limits last for only 24 hours, though some may be prepared to accept longer instructions of this sort.

Once the transaction is complete the broker sends a contract note detailing the deal and how much money is to change hands. It may take some time to receive the share certificate, but that is incidental since it is your presence on the share register that really determines ownership of the holding. The inconveniences can be circumvented by having the broker keep the holdings in a 'nominee' account or by having them electronically registered in Crest.

11 | How do you find out the cost of a share?

There are nearly 3,000 companies quoted on the London stock exchange, some with several types of issues, plus the Alternative Investment Market (Aim), TechMARK, and Ofex (see Chapter 20). The majority of quoted companies are traded infrequently, with the greatest volume of interest and trade being in the 100 largest companies by market value. These are the components of the FTSE 100 Share Index. The FTSE 100 is the main indicator of trends in the stock market currently in use. Its name is an abbreviation of the Financial Times Stock Exchange 100, devised between the *Financial Times* newspaper and the actuarial profession. The reason for the pre-eminence of the FTSE (often referred to as the 'Footsie') is partly because the major companies in it represent a significant portion of Britain's industry and exports, and their importance in the investment strategy of major financial institutions. The concentration of institutional interest in those companies is shown most clearly when there is a change in the composition of that Index. This happens when an already large company takes on a spurt in market value, while at the same time a couple of others are not doing as well as they used to or have become unfashionable for some obscure reason. Then there is a shuffle and the constituents of the FTSE change to ensure it continues to include the largest 100 companies by value. The moment a company drops out of the Index its shares take a sudden fall, sometimes by as much as 5 per cent, while conversely the new member of the elite gains a sudden additional jump.

Below that top level is the next tier down, made up of the next 250 companies measured once again by market capitalization – that is, in both these categories it is not turnover, profit, asset value or any other measure that counts, merely the aggregate value of the issued shares.

NEWSPAPERS

All these 350 largest companies are in the lists of the broadsheet newspapers' prices pages, which also contain several hundred other companies. But none of the papers has the space to show all the securities available. Even the *Financial Times,* which devotes more pages than the others to share prices, can show only part of the list actually quoted.

Newspapers display a range of other information as well, including how the share price moved from the closing of the previous day and so on (see Chapter 13). The price of shares in the big companies is moving continuously. The morning newspaper will give the closing price of the previous night, but by the time you read it the cost of the shares will almost certainly be different. To compound the problem, the price printed is the mid-market price. That is the average of the buying and selling prices.

ONLINE

The advent of the Internet means we are no longer dependent on the morning paper to bring us (slightly out of date) information, nor do we have to be a major institution to get a current share price. Many of the online brokers (see Chapter 10) offer price information to clients and some have 'real-time' prices (the ones being quoted at that moment on the exchange computers), occasionally for an additional subscription.

It can be convenient to have the price and other services through the one screen address, but there are places on the Net where the price information is available for nothing. One example is www.investment-gateway.com, which has a range of free services.

THE SPREAD

Anybody who has bought holiday money knows the price of buying is always higher than the price at which you can sell, with that spread depending on the trader and what you are buying or selling.

It is the same with shares. The difference – the so-called spread – will depend on a range of factors that affect the dealer's risk. One is what the market calls liquidity: how many shares there are available and how many people are prepared to trade in them. A good measure as far as the stock market is concerned is how much the price moves when you try to trade. Try to buy shares in a company with few on issue and most of those locked up by holders not prepared to be tempted out by a small rise in the value, and the price will suddenly bounce.

Massive companies like British Telecom, Vodafone, etc, have millions of shares on issue and there is always somebody in the market wanting to deal in them. By contrast a relatively small business with a market capitalization of £10 million, of which the chairman owns half and his family and directors own another quarter, with most of the rest held by the initial investors, makes it very difficult. Its size means few people have heard about the business, so not many want to deal in the shares, and even if they did want to it could be quite tricky to find a counter-party. So the first will have a relatively narrow spread because the more trade there is in a share the more confident the dealer is of getting shot of any, while the latter will probably have a frighteningly wide spread.

The width of the spread also depends on the state of the market. In wildly fluctuating shares, market-makers are loath to stick their necks out and carefully widen the spread. So the mid-market price is just an indication of the actual rate the shares will fetch in a real deal.

People who deal over the telephone can ask the broker, who will look at the stock exchange screen showing all the people dealing in the shares and their prices. The broker can specify exactly what the price is then and if the agreement is swift may be able to deal at that price. An alternative is to get access to the prices pages via the Internet and check the prices for oneself.

In the largest companies a different system is used. People wanting to deal, feed their orders into the computer via the broker, complete with the size of the order and whether they are buyers or sellers. They can also add a caveat that they want to deal 'at best', which means the deal is put through immediately at the best price available; or they can set a limit (the maximum a buyer is prepared to pay, the minimum a seller is prepared to accept). Another choice is 'fill or kill', which is combined with a limit price – that means at least some of the deal is done immediately or it is cancelled, but if part of it is dealt the rest is wiped.

This operates only for the largest companies and is put through the Sets computers (the London 'Stock Exchange Electronic Trading System'), which should therefore eliminate the spread and in theory reduce the cost of trading.

WHY AT THAT PRICE?

The actual level of share prices is only the start, though. One also needs to know why the price is at that level. For this there is the financial press (see Chapter 12), and also the other sources of information and advice (see Chapter 18). In addition there is information available from stockbrokers, and people who are paying for advice should have a steady flow of guidance.

The Internet is overflowing with information, some of it accurate, a little of it useful. Among the reliable and often helpful sources there is the worldwide news agency Bloomberg, City-wire, and some online brokers who have company data and other services available at their sites.

12 | What do the newspaper financial pages mean?

The number of newspaper pages devoted to business, investment and money has been growing steadily for many years. In addition to the increasing bulk of City pages in the daily papers, weekend newspapers have expanded so much they now separate the business part from the personal finance. On top of that there are a large number of business and investment magazines, ranging from the venerable *Investors Chronicle* to upwards of another half-dozen others. In addition to general business journals like *Fortune*, *Forbes* and *Business Week* (all American), there are magazines such as *Your Money*, *Money Management*, *Moneywise*, *Personal Finance*, *Bloomberg Money*, *Shares* and *Money Observer*.

There are several reference books, like *REFS*, *UK Major Companies Handbook*, and *UK Smaller Companies Handbook*, which provide statistics and facts about business and companies. These are on top of the guides to the stock exchange and other investments, plus other explanations of the financial markets. (See Further reading at the end of this book.)

Although the personal or family finance pages are generally written in language that does not require a degree in economics, the main City pages have quite a lot of material that presupposes years of experience.

PRICES PAGES – DURING THE WEEK

Let us start with the simple part, the pages showing share prices. Broadsheet newspapers have companies listed under the market sectors to which they have been allocated; they will also be a constituent of that part or heading of the FT-Actuaries sector index. It is rather confusing that not all the newspapers label the sectors using the same words. The choice of sector is not always obvious and some companies feel they are in the wrong group – especially when that group becomes unfashionable – so occasionally there is a change of allocation by the Stock Exchange authorities, though that tends to happen when the company itself has altered the emphasis of its work.

High	Low	Stock	Price	–	Yld	P/E
90	56^{1}4	Kidde♦	84^{1}2	+1^{1}2	1.8	19.4
18^{1}4	7^{1}2	Locker	9^{1}4	...	12.4	25.7
41^{1}2	23	MS Intl	39	...	3.4	–
195^{1}2	88^{1}2	Mang Bronze ..	112^{1}2	...	c9.8	6.5
142^{1}2	73	Mayflower	100	+1^{1}2	4.0	21.3
76	48	McLeod Russ ..	59^{1}2*–^{1}2		c11.9	12.2
282	172	Meggitt♦	245	+3^{1}2	2.6	19.4
79^{1}2	59	Metalrax	75	...	7.2	9.0
187^{1}2	110	Molins	179	–^{1}2	1.7	9.6
337	223^{1}2	Morgan Cru♦ .	314	–6^{1}2	5.1	12.5
119^{1}2	70	Precoat Intnl ...	70	...	8.9	6.4
122^{1}2	81^{1}2	Renold	104	–^{1}2	8.9	9.9
250	161	**Rolls Royce**	234^{1}2	–3^{1}2	3.4	44.0
377^{1}2	218	Rotork	356^{1}2	–1	3.4	22.9
72	41^{1}2	Senior	65^{1}2	+^{1}2	7.5	–
298	182^{1}2	Severfield R	277^{1}2	...	5.0	8.6
83	52^{1}2	600 Group	71^{1}2	–^{1}2	7.7	7.4
984	632	**Smiths Group** ..	835	+^{1}2	2.9	14.9
501^{1}2	329	Spirax Sarco ...	488^{1}2	–^{1}2	3.7	13.8
35^{1}2	10	Stratagem	21^{1}4	–^{1}4	–	–
95^{1}2	61	Syltone	78^{1}2	...	9.4	31.3
165^{1}2	90^{1}2	Tex Hldgs.	96^{1}2	+5	7.8	8.6

Figure 12.1   The *Daily Telegraph*'s share prices page during the week

Company name, etc

The third column shows the company name, sometimes in abbreviated form, and if its shares were not issued in sterling the currency is also given. Almost always what is quoted is the ordinary share (called 'common stock' in the United States), but some companies issue other quoted paper (see Chapter 2), such as irredeemable preference stock, convertibles, warrants and so on, and these are normally listed underneath. The one most often traded is indicated with a ☐ in the *Financial Times*. Sometimes there are additional symbols. For instance, in the *FT*:

A alongside a share name often indicates it carries no voting rights, but that is sometimes made more explicit by adding N/V;

♣ indicates that investors can get a free copy of the company's latest report and accounts;

♥ says the stock is not officially listed in Britain, which generally speaking means it is a foreign mining company;

♠ indicates an unregulated collective investment scheme;

xd means the recently declared dividend will still be paid to the previous owner of the share;

xr indicates the same for a rights issue – ie the buyer will not be acquiring the right to subscribe to the new issue of shares;

xc means the buyer does not get scrip issue of shares which the company is distributing in lieu of a dividend (xc because the official name is a capitalization issue; see the Glossary at the end of this book).

In *The Daily Telegraph*:

bold type like this indicates it is one the 100 largest companies, a member of the FTSE 100 Index;

◆ says the company is one of the next 250 largest, and so a member of the FTSE Mid 250 Index;

* says the shares are quoted ex-dividend;

† ex-scrip;

§ is ex-rights;

‡ is ex-all;

\# shows trading in the shares has been suspended;

A means the annual report and accounts are due soon.

Closing price

The fourth column gives the closing price of the share the previous night or the last trading day. As with all goods there is a higher buying and a lower selling price, the difference between them being the 'spread'. What the newspapers quote is the average of those two, called the mid-market price, when trade stopped the previous night. So no investor can hope to buy at the price or sell at it, even if the market had not moved by the time the newspaper arrives through the letterbox. If trading in the shares has been suspended – say because the company is being reorganized, or there are questions about the figures, or because it is subject to a takeover – the price listed is the last one before suspension, with # next to it.

Price change

The fifth column shows the price change from the previous day's closing level, also at the mid-market price.

52-week high/low

This column shows the highs and lows the share price has reached over the previous year overall – in other words, unlike the previous figures these are the actual figures reached during the day's trading and may not be the price at which the shares closed the day's trading. That will then indicate whether the share is near its maximum or minimum. So if the share price is currently 127p and the highs and lows are 123p and 478p, you can immediately tell that the price is very near the bottom level it has reached in the past year.

Volume

Volume of trade gives an indication of how many thousands of shares changed hands on the previous trading day. The figure is the total of equities bought and sold – in other words there is double counting. The figure shows the level of interest in the company's shares and is an indication of the liquidity in the market. It is salutary to see how many were not dealt in at all. Some newspapers print a separate table of the previous day's most highly traded shares.

Yield

Yield is the percentage return provided at the share price listed in the table and at the current rate of dividends. The formula is: multiply the annual gross dividend by 100, and then divide by the share's market price. So if the shares cost 200p and the latest year's dividend was 14p, the yield is 7 per cent. This is normally reported gross, ie before tax has been deducted, though almost everybody gets the dividend cheques net and the tax is not reclaimable.

The *Daily Telegraph* prices pages print the letter b to indicate that the interim dividend has been raised; c means the interim dividend has been reduced or it has been omitted altogether.

P/E

The P/E stands for price/earnings ratio, and is probably the best-known method of assessing equities. It is calculated by comparing the current share price with the level of earnings per share (found in the company's accounts – see Chapter 14).

The company's accounts may say something like, 'attributable to ordinary shareholders £850,000' and at the bottom of the profit and loss table it will say something like, 'earnings on each of the 10 million shares on issue 8½p'. To get the P/E ratio you divide this 8½ into the prevailing market price of the shares. If this stands at, say, 170p then $170/8½ = 20$. If the share price then halves to 85p the P/E ratio would be 10 and if the shares shot up to 255p the P/E would be 30.

One can then inspect the other companies in the same industry sector of the paper and see how they compare. If most of the companies are on a P/E of between 12 and 16 and one of the companies is on 25, either the market knows great things are on the way from it, or the shares are grossly overpriced. Conversely, if all of the sector is on a P/E of 18 to 20 and one of the companies is on 4, either the market knows there is some nasty news on the way from the management or they are wrong and the shares are grossly underpriced.

NAV

Instead of price/earnings ratios, the column for investment trusts (see Chapter 6) shows NAV, which stands for net asset value. That is a calculation of the investment trust's holdings as a value per share. Like the share price, it is quoted in pence. The *Financial Times* also has a column showing 'Dis or Pm (-)'. That is a calculation of the difference between the net asset value and the actual price of the share – Dis means the shares are at a discount as the price is below the asset value; Pm means the shares are at a premium to the underlying value of the investments. Perversely and confusingly a discount is shown as a positive figure, while a premium is shown with a minus sign.

The Association of Investment Trust Companies (AITC) also produces a monthly booklet on the prices and details of other figures of its members (see Useful addresses at the end of this book).

Gilts

There are also prices tables for gilts – government-issued securities (see Chapter 3). These are usually split into short, medium and long-dated. There are also the two undated ones, and index-linked stocks. Foreign governments also issue bonds that are obtainable and quoted in the UK, sometimes with a lower yield than native varieties. See Figure 12.2 on page 68.

Unit trusts

The heading of the prices pages is actually 'Unit Trusts and Open-Ended Investment Companies Prices'. The various units are grouped under the management company, such as Aberdeen, M&G and so on, with the addresses and telephone numbers so one can call for application forms and information – investors do not have to go through stockbrokers to buy them but can go direct to the companies, some of which also have regular savings plans. Some of the companies list several phone numbers for trading, information, prices and so on. With the name some of them also have a number in figures. For instance, Abbey National UT Managers Ltd has next to it (1200) F; which means the prices

52 week				+ or	Yield	
High	Low	Stock	Price	–	Flat	Rm@
£101.37	£100.59	Treas 7% 2001	£100.59	−0.02	6.96	5.23
£104.05	£101.45	Treas 7% 2002	£101.48	+0.01	6.90	5.35
£107.44	£104.77	Treas. 9¾% 2002 .	£104.80	*+0.01	9.30	5.39
£106.58	£104.44	Treas 8% 2003	£104.53	+0.01	7.66	5.51
£112.02	£11.16	Treas 10% 2003	£109.09	+0.01	9.17	5.52
£104.27	£101.57	Treas 6½% 2003 ..	£102.37	...	6.35	5.46
£100.66	£97.13	Treas 5% 2004	£98.72	...	5.08	5.36
£96.57	£92.57	Fndg 3½% 99–04 .	£94.82	...	3.69	5.39
£106.70	£103.54	Treas 6¾% 2004 ..	£103.88	...	6.50	5.49
£115.69	£111.56	Treas 8½ 2005	£111.68	+0.01	7.61	5.50
£117.29	£113.21	Conv 9½% 2005 ...	£113.32	...	8.38	5.56
£1110.10	£109.11	Treas 7½% 06	£109.46	...	6.86	5.47
£114.13	£109.91	Treas 7¾% 06	£110.01	...	7.05	5.51
£104.56	£103.07	Treas 8% 02/06	£103.11	+0.01	7.76	5.41
£120.11	£106.38	Treas 8½% 2007 ..	£115.31	−0.01	7.38	5.49
£114.31	£109.32	Treas 7¼% 2007 ..	£109.62	...	6.62	5.46
£127.00	£121.10	Treas 9% 2008	£121.11	−0.02	7.44	5.46
£107.99	£102.51	Treas 5¾ 2009	£102.51	−0.02	5.61	5.39
£113.35	£106.68	Treas.6¼% 2010 ..	£106.68	−0.10	5.87	5.35
£136.86	£121.26	Conv 9% 2011	£128.53	*−0.06	7.01	5.31
£139.27	£130.20	Treas 9% 2012	£130.20	*−0.13	6.92	5.37
£105.22	£99.58	Tr~~e~~ ~~5~~½% 08–12	£100.7~~3~~ ~~–0~~.03		5.46	5.39
£132.19	£123.38	~~Tr~~ 2013	£123.~~9~~ ~~8~~		6.49	5.38
£125.5~~9~~			£1~~~~			.51

Figure 12.2 Newspaper tables for gilt-edged stock have slightly different information to share prices pages

were set at noon (it is worked on a 24-hour clock) and the company uses forward pricing – orders are taken from investors and the price is determined from the next valuation (see Chapter 9).

Noon is the most common time for setting prices. This means that an investor telephoning an order at 11 am would be buying at a price set an hour later, but another one calling at 1 pm would have to wait until the next day for the price.

The 52-week highs and lows are similar to those for shares, but for unit trusts the papers print a buying and selling price and a change in the mid-market price from the previous ones. Some also provide a column to show yield gross as a percentage of the offer price (at which the investor buys).

MONDAYS

On Mondays, with no news on the trading front (readers will presumably have got the week's closing prices from the Saturday newspaper, if not off the Net), the newspapers have the chance to print different or additional material.

Market capitalization

Market capitalization is the total value of the company on the stock market at the current share price. So if Consolidated Alaskan Coconut Plantations has issued 50 million shares and they are currently being traded at 85p, then the company is valued at £42.5 million at the moment and that is how much it would cost to buy all its shares. This is of no help in deciding whether it is a good buy or not, but newspapers have always printed the figure and it does at least give some indication of its standing.

If the company is in the FTSE 100, then it is one of the largest companies in the country, and you can gauge the market rating by combinations of price/earnings ratio, yield and market capitalization (see Chapter 15). Do not be fooled by size though – Polly Peck was once a huge company in the FTSE 100 Index just before imploding when the man who ran it jumped bail to flee to Northern Cyprus.

Other data

There is also information like the percentage change of price during the week, the last dividend (usually shown net of tax), when it was last quoted xd (ex-dividend); ◀ in the *Financial Times* indicates an increase in the interim dividend in the current financial year and ☐ shows a decrease; dividend cover (see Chapter 15) shows the number of times that level of dividend could have been paid out of the latest profits. There is often a separate table for the most recent issues.

INDICES

The newspapers also print figures for the movement of industrial sectors such as engineering and machinery, plus some describing the type of share such as small cap (small total market value of the shares). These are then aggregated to form still wider industrial indices such as Basic Industries, General Industrials, 650, All Share (which does not in fact include all shares) and so on. The

Financial Times produces a full list of the FTSE indices compiled and calculated under formulae developed by actuaries.

In the *Daily Telegraph* there are two tables of indices on the prices page. One is for the 12 largest foreign stock markets, with the exception of New York and Toronto, which are in the Key Markets table on the facing page (the owner of the newspaper is Canadian), though Tokyo's Nikkei Index appears on both pages. The other table shows the major British share indices including the FTSE 100 and 250 (plus the 350 which is just those two together) and the 30, which was the FTSE 100's predecessor. There is also the Techmark, which is the stock market's attempt to show backing for the newcomers in high technology by separating them into a go-go index, which has turned into a bit of a go-stop-go.

Every stock market has its indices to indicate market movement as a whole. Different papers report different selections of these. Some of the better known ones are the Dow Jones, Nasdaq, Standard & Poor's, Toronto 300, Nikkei, Hang Seng, Dax for Germany, CAC40 for France and the Toronto Composite Index. There is also a table of the highest volumes of trade.

EDITORIAL

In addition to the tables (and in tabloids generally instead of them), there are the articles. The financial pages carry some broad economic news but in the main their focus of interest is on news about companies. These items contain vital information to investors who try to take seriously the job of finding a good share. The news pages carry stories not just about takeovers and other dramatic events but also have interviews with the top managers. In addition, they carry details of plans, new products, investments, any change of tactics, recruitment of new senior staff, changes at board level, sales of subsidiaries and a host of other indications of how a company is approaching its business. In the course of these articles journalists usually give strong hints about how the management and products of a company are regarded. That gives an added layer of information to the investor.

In addition, the plain and fairly brief reproduction of results from smaller or less interesting companies, which concentrates on turnover, profit and exceptional items plus directors' pay, there are columns that concentrate on analysing financial results published that day by companies – eg, Questor, Lex and Tempus. These columns do not always make explicit recommendations to buy or sell, but the general message of their comments is usually obvious.

People have a tendency to say they believe nothing they read in newspapers, but then act as if journalists were omniscient supermen. Journalists know only what somebody has told them, and though the good ones do conscientiously dig behind the facts and try to interpret and test what they hear, they are fallible like the rest of us. They do however mix in the City world, talk to all the people who are directly and indirectly involved and keep an eye on what is going on. Anybody getting into investments would be foolish to lose out on the flood of information that is available. There is daily detail on a wide variety of companies and sectors, discussing the managers, products, performance, deals and prospects. Some of it may be nothing but gossip or a space-filler, but in the reputable press there is often more and better informed early news about what is happening than comes out of stockbrokers. In addition, the more authoritative writers do get read and as a result may move public opinion about a company and hence the share price.

An increasing amount of this information is available via the Internet. This includes electronic versions of the newspapers such as the *Daily Telegraph* at www.telegraph.co.uk, the *Financial Times* at www.ft.com and the weekly magazine *Investors Chronicle* at www.investorschronicle.com. In addition, there are news services such as www.bloomberg.com. Then there are specialist services such as www.thestreet.com.

With so many broadsheet pages devoted every day to the City, company news and investment, plus the heavy Sunday papers' big financial sections, as well as a number of magazines such as the *Investors Chronicle* concentrating on investment advice, it is hard to see what the tip sheets can add.

13 | How do you pick a share to buy?

Warning: almost everyone who has ever had anything to do with the stock market has a theory of how to pick a share. They are similar to addicted gamblers and their sure-fire systems for winning at roulette or horseracing. The bookshops are bulging with pet schemes and private formulae. Those winning methods come in predictable categories. There are the strategic views, which range from in-and-out trading all the time, to buy and forget, and there is the tactical advice category, which shows the infallible way to pick the best bet.

As is being repeatedly emphasized in this book, beware of all advice. Do not immediately reject it, but just remember nobody gets it right all the time. And even the people who do get it right more often than not, do not really know how they do it – their explanations are usually post-hoc rationalization as they struggle to explain just what instinct drove them to buy that or sell the other at just the right time. If by some chance they really could formulate the trick, they would be very foolish to share the secret with the rest of us and so queer the pitch for themselves.

Judging by the proliferation of such books there is clearly more money to be made from publishing accounts of a wonderful new way of making a fortune on the stock market than from putting the principle to work and buying shares. Why otherwise would all those people be so diligently occupied writing and getting people to compete with them in searching for the routes to fortune, when they could be researching the market and dealing?

The point for an investor is to absorb all the information available, but to weigh it carefully and always to test it against common sense. Some of the advice available is sensible and helpful, some less so. Following someone else's method slavishly will probably not work, but some combination of the methods described in this chapter should be able to help most people evolve their own way of approaching a challenging but personal task.

PET SYSTEMS

Even the famously successful Warren Buffett claims to have a formula (if you can call it that, so wonderfully simple is it), but it is not very obviously helpful to the novice investor. When pressed, his advice was to buy good businesses and hang on to them. Admirers have written lengthy books about him and this easily comprehensible, if hard to achieve, system.

The businessman Richard Koch had a more elaborate version, though it was probably saying much the same thing. He said follow the known successes in investment, buy companies with a good trading record, specialize, watch profit trends, stick to companies with good business reputations, pick companies that generate lots of cash and produce a high return on capital, risk part of the portfolio on emerging markets, sell any share that has dropped by at least 8 per cent.

The American investor Michael O'Higgins reckons you should select the 10 highest-yielding shares in the index, and then pick the five with the lowest share price.

Malcolm Stacey, the author of one of these investment guides, advises spreading the money among sectors, buying slow but steady risers, and sticking to leaders (including ones in their sector). He also has the 'filter rule', which aims to catch a share before it reaches a new stable higher value or drops to a new lower one, by setting a price differential at which dealing is triggered – if the filter were set at 10 per cent, then every time the share fell 10 per cent off a peak one should sell, and start buying again when it came 10 per cent off the bottom.

T Rowe Price launched a fund in the 1950s and set out his principles in a book, *Principles of Growth Stock Valuation*. His advice was to concentrate on companies with a long-term earnings

growth record and the chances of continuing that way, which he defined as reaching a new peak at the top of each business cycle. You can pick these, he reckons, by finding an industry where unit sales and profits are rising, and a company with good patents, products and management.

Peter Lynch ran the Magellan fund in the 1980s and, not content with having made his fortune through that good period, decided to tell us how to emulate him in a book called *Beating the Street*.

Jim Slater has the 'Zulu Principle', which he has published in a couple of books. And so on and on and on.

Even the two journalists who had to resign from the *Daily Mirror* after there had been staff dealings prior to their recommendations in the paper have produced a guide called *Make a Million in Twelve Months*. Their system, though straightforward, takes a lot of work: it includes picking small companies with lowly priced shares and ignoring what they actually do as irrelevant. It also involves absorbing enormous amounts of market information, including such details as job advertisements that might indicate the company's direction and fortunes.

Many of these people advocating systems have themselves been successful, but note how varied the advice is. So beware of formulae, and be especially wary of fashionable investment gurus.

SETTING CRITERIA

The reason other people's systems will probably not work for you is that all investment strategies are in fact rationalized feel and judgement and most goodish ones require lots of hard work. There is no certain and predictable scheme for making money or everybody would have been using it long since.

That is not a recipe for despair. Although borrowed tactics will not produce infallible opulence, there are some common-sense ways of looking at companies and their shares that will increase the chances of success. This is serious stuff however, and an investor who hopes to make money out of the stock market will have to make an effort. Everything has a price, and the cost of making money is usually hard graft. People like Warren Buffett did not get rich by accident or by following a secret trick; he thinks, eats, breathes and sleeps the stock market. He may not be the world's wittiest and most wide-ranging conversationalist, but then you have to ask yourself just how seriously you want to be rich, or even slightly better off.

MARKET THEORIES

Against all that theorizing and system creation is a countervailing view which, in its strictest formulation, says the effort is futile. Some serious people have analysed the markets and have produced academically respectable theses to prove that any attempt to outperform the average is doomed to failure – it is just not possible, they say. They have produced the 'random walk' theory, which says movements of prices are inherently unpredictable in both size and direction, and as a result any wins or losses are purely a matter of chance. In the long run you will end up even, or at least will have moved with the market as whole.

Another hypothesis, which also asserts that trying to outperform the market is a waste of time, says the market is efficient, in the economists' sense – it incorporates in the share price all the available knowledge. That means all the information about the company, economic prospects and the market are pretty well universally disseminated – everybody has access to the same information – and there are no people with enough financial clout to move the market. As a result, the price of shares already reflects the concerted and probably relatively accurate view of the totality of investors, private and institutional. Since shares have no 'correct' price, runs this hypothesis, and are worth only what somebody is prepared to pay for them, the general consensus view is the 'right' price and the shares are unlikely to move away from it. In any case, this is likely to reflect the underlying truth as well, because of that widely available information about the business.

The inevitable conclusion of such theories is that getting it right is a matter of luck not judgement. Some people may get it right more often than not, but that is only in the short term and is part of the normal statistical fluctuation and will not last.

Fine in theory, but even the most cursory glance will show the stock market to be anything but random and a long way from being rational. There are anomalies, and not everyone has reacted yet to the information that can be gleaned. Information may be available but not everybody has taken it on board. For instance, keeping an eye on advertisements for high-powered jobs may show a company about to move into or enlarging an important area (such as the Internet) but not everybody does vet such ads, so the information is not generally known.

In addition, the market does not act in line with the economists' depiction of optimizing behaviour. The swings seem to demonstrate frequent overreaction, amounting at times to hysteria or blind herd stampedes, and it is clear some people do have a shrewder appreciation of what is going on than others. If it were an efficient market, making it therefore impossible consistently to do better than the average, how do you explain people who have actually made themselves – and sometimes their clients – a major fortune? There are some notable names who have steadily made money and some famous investment managers who have over a long term performed about five to six times as well as the market as a whole.

A plain indication that the perfect market is some way off comes from the most cursory of looks at the views of stockbrokers' analysts on company shares – there is little general agreement about the prospective performance of many companies. The price cannot have incorporated all these views because they contradict each other. And as the old saying goes, two views make a market.

The academics are therefore modifying their views and conceding there may be pockets of inefficiency that continue to exist and which could provide the sharp analyst with an opportunity. Market practitioners have also pointed out that this sort of rigid academic picture depends on the timescale – in the very short term movements in prices may seem random and irrational but the longer you extend the period the more logical it becomes (which is the incentive for the 'fundamental' analyst – see below).

So the effort is not wholly wasted, and it may be indispensable to prevent making disastrous mistakes, though beating the market is not going to be easy.

SHARE ANALYSIS

Fundamental analysis

In deciding what share to buy and when, the first thing to remember is that there is no absolute or correct price. Fundamental analysis may provide some answers on what the underlying value can be said to be and what dividend flow is probable or at least possible, but that may no more move the price in future than in the past. In other words the price is moved by market reaction, so it is pointless to keep saying one must buy a company's shares because they are undervalued by the market, as shown by the business being on, for instance, a lower price/earnings ratio than other companies in its sector with less stable finances. If the market continues to undervalue the business, the shares will not move higher.

The assumption behind doing this work on a company is that the market has developed only a temporary blindness or misjudgement and will in due course come to appreciate true value. In other words, the thought is that the exercise is worth it because whatever fads and follies shunt the market in the short term, eventually value will be recognized. So one is aiming to pick winners not yet spotted by others.

This is the province of fundamental analysis, which looks at the business and products of the company and its published accounts; examines things like earnings and dividends prospects; takes account of the economic ambience such as the rate of inflation, the level of sterling, consumer demand and interest levels; watches the market it is in and what the competition is up to; and judges the company's management. It then decides whether the business is fairly valued by the market.

Assuming the analyst is right and way ahead of the rest of the market, a correction could still take years, during which time the company could be so seriously hampered by its low share price that its business is overtaken by competitors. So fundamental analysis will show whether the market values a company unfairly, but before buying you still need to be sure it will soon see its mistake. The obvious question is how can anyone foretell that, and there is no simple answer. This is where market feel comes in – the result of all that reading of the financial press, listening to the radio, etc, and good instincts. Some people just feel there will be an imminent shift in attitudes to a specific company, an industrial sector, or a type of company, but the more you know and the harder you work the luckier you will be.

Bear in mind that you are not alone in this quest. There are droves of analysts being paid ludicrous amounts of money to help institutions beat the market, plus millions of private investors on the hunt for the end of the same rainbow. As a result, the prices in the main reflect the sum of their expectations both about the company and the market in which it operates. In other words, they set the price not on what it is doing now but what it is likely to be doing over the next couple of years – the price has discounted the future. The search therefore is for anomalies.

Fundamental analysis concentrates on the true value of a company and then checks whether the share price reflects that. These calculations are described in Chapter 15. Nearly all these calculations are done from published accounts. One can learn an awful lot about a company from reading its annual report and accounts. They are filed at Companies House, but most companies will send a copy to prospective investors if asked nicely.

The accounts reveal not just what the formulae calculate, but a wealth of other information. Elaborate financial engineering, suggestions of skilful burnishing of results, or careful reallocation of figures are all signs that the business is not all it seems or the management is a touch flaky. Either way, characteristics to avoid.

City analysts are already doing most of these calculations, but they are always looking ahead, so the price discounts the expectation of the next announcement. That is the reason incidentally why shares sometimes act paradoxically, falling on the publication of good trading figures or rising after a mediocre result: the market has already factored in those numbers and after publication is reassessing the shares in the light of the next set of results. If you think the market has got its expectations wrong it is possible to trade in the hope of a sharp reaction when the true figures come out, if they are in line with your projections. This still requires not only that you are right, but that the rest of the market views the new information in the way you have expected.

For instance, a company may be producing pretty comfortable levels of profit and yet its shares fail to respond appropriately. That could be because the market reckons that further down the road there is trouble looming, or because the company is just too small to interest the institutional investing funds, or because the price has already reflected just that level of profit, or even because the company may be good but the sector is currently out of favour.

All this discussion assumes an investor is trying to do better than the market as a whole. It is not the only strategy. Many individuals and hordes of investment funds reckon the task is too fraught and opt for the safer course of just trying to keep the investments as good as the market as a whole. Since on a longer term the market trend is generally upwards, this is a safe and lower-risk approach.

If, however, you are going to try to beat the market, where do you find the shares currently neglected, but which will be spotted as the rising stars of the future? It clearly cannot be from a comprehensive scrutiny of company reports, because with nearly 3,000 UK companies to choose from (not to mention the increasingly accessible overseas markets), the prospect looks a touch daunting. Even if you exclude large numbers of them, such as the biggest 350 because they are so extensively covered by stockbrokers' analysts as to leave little room for the amateur, and you omit 'shell' companies and businesses which are evidently incomprehensible (never buy the shares of a company if its business seems odd or its income inexplicable), you still have a formidably large area of research.

For the private investor the answer is to create a set of personal filters. This can be by sticking to companies with a P/E ratio of no more than five or six, or with a yield at least 10 per cent above the average. It can be by looking at neglected sectors: is it fair that retailing should be under such a cloud; is manufacturing still going through those troubles that made professional investors shun them; are breweries really a better bet than catering companies; and so on. In a sense it is being the counter-cyclical investor. Then one selects from that long list the companies that may appeal for other reasons.

The best approach is to combine all the information that you have gathered with the other criteria available, such as a look at the country's economy (some types of company do better on an upturn and some survive downturns better), the shopper's view and technical analysis (see below).

'Shell' and recovery stocks

One area for potentially spectacular changes of fortune is 'shell' and recovery companies. They require a specialized form of forecasting. 'Shell' companies have little or no existing business but are clinging to a continued stock market listing. Their purpose is to act as a cheap way for another company to get a stock market quotation. Some sharp managers can move in, raise money to acquire other companies (possibly private), or another business can get onto the exchange by a 'reverse takeover' – the quoted company is legally buying the unquoted but is in reality taken over by the unquoted one's managers and business.

Some people therefore reckon shell companies provide a good cheap punt. That may be so, but on the other hand, you really do not know what will happen or who will be in charge, so it is a gamble unless through having a careful ear to the ground you have picked up whispers.

A parallel problem is with 'recovery' stocks. This approach says a company has suffered a bad period and is on the mend, or even that a company doctor has moved in to heal its ills. Get the prediction right and the investment is likely to bring rapid returns, but history shows the odds are against you. As Warren Buffett said, 'When a company with a reputation for incompetence meets a new management with a reputation for competence, it is the reputation of the company that is likely to remain intact.'

That is a sobering thought from an acknowledged winner, but it is not always true. Stumbling companies have been rescued from the edge of the abyss by company doctors or revised policies. In addition, though the stock market may show disgust, the profits could be down for some very good reason: the company has invested a massive amount into research and development for a series of new products that will create huge new markets; it has bought a new business which will extend its own range; it has restructured the company to be more efficient (including expensive redundancies); and so on. It is always worth looking behind facts for causes. There may be the seeds of hope, or Buffett could be right and the loser will sink into oblivion.

The converse does not hold true, as recent years have demonstrated all too clearly. Winners do not hold their top place for ever. Gerald Ratner was said to be able to defy gravity and have his share price rise while all other retailers groaned with pain. Then, triggered perhaps by a foolish joke in public about the goods he sold, the price plummeted so fast he himself could not retain his boardroom seat or the jewellery chain with his name on the fascia. Sainsbury's and Marks & Spencer were for a long time revered as the retailers with the magic touch, and it seemed they could do no wrong – until they seemed in the eyes of the market to do everything wrong and their shares tumbled.

One can detect the same thing more generally across the market. Shares that performed best between 1982 and 1992 included Guinness (which subsequently became Diageo), Hanson (which dropped out of the FTSE 100 in the spring of 2000), Courtaulds (which never did as well again and eight years later was finally put out of its misery by a takeover), and ICI (which later struggled and tried to stop the rot by splitting itself in two and selling off subsidiaries, but languished).

Bearing all those factors in mind, one can then begin to set the criteria for an investment policy that relies less on hunch and hope and a little more on a realistic appraisal of personal needs and market circumstances.

Technical analysis

The normal contrast to fundamental analysis is chartism, also called technical analysis. This is concerned exclusively with the movements of share prices in the recent past to forecast how they will move in future. The really dedicated chartist does not even enquire whether the price chart he is looking at is for houses, airline tickets, gold bars, or the shares of banks, because he maintains the information is all in the pattern of movements.

So the main point of this is in complete contrast with fundamental analysis: it totally ignores the underlying worth of the business. Technical analysis is concerned not with whether the company is efficiently managed but with when the market price is likely to change. The work consists in plotting the share price in a variety of different ways to see if there is a pattern developing which indicates a more substantial movement.

This means it can in theory be used for screening price movements to find promising indicators and signs of really spectacular changes in market attitudes. In practice, it is rather more commonly used as a supplementary guide – it can suggest your hunch was right and the market really is about to reassess an undervalued business; or it can merely indicate when the time is best for dealing in a share you had already picked for a variety of other reasons: an indication not of what but of when (see Chapters 18 and 26).

The shopper's view

One relatively sensible and straightforward way of reducing the number of potential companies to examine is to buy the shares of businesses whose products and services seem good. For instance, if shopping at Sainsbury's has become expensive and a pain and you are going to Tesco instead, or vice versa, a similar view may strike other shoppers, and eventually the profits and share price will reflect that. Similarly if you have come across a product or service that seems outstanding as well as providing good value, and the company behind it seems sound and ambitious, it may in due course become a darling of the stock market.

PERSONAL PRIORITIES

It is just as well that there are so many quoted securities and so many ways of selecting them because everybody has a different set of preferences.

Some people want to invest long term – buy the shares, stick them away and wait for retirement. Some people like to catch the passing market eddies and nip in and out of the market as prices fluctuate. Some thrive on risk if there is a chance of big rewards, and some would be kept awake at nights by the very thought of endangering their savings. Some want a good steady income, and some would prefer to concentrate on capital appreciation as the value of the shares increases.

These are decisions you cannot shuck off onto someone else. Even if the portfolio is to be managed by a professional, the conversation will start with these basic criteria:

▌ the investment horizon;
▌ the level of acceptable risk;
▌ the need for income;
▌ ethical considerations.

One way not to pick shares is to allow some salesman to foist them on you by hard selling. It is illegal under British law, but there are overseas brokers ringing people up touting no-loss investments. They are very persuasive, quote the performance of their previous recommendations, and may offer a money-back guarantee. Take the name and number of the person and pass it on to the Financial Services Authority.

Setting guidelines

One way of screening the thousands of potential investments is to set your own goals clearly and explicitly. It is not nearly enough to say the aim is to make money out of the stock exchange. The process means setting a time horizon for the investment; the amount of risk one is prepared to live with; deciding whether the investment is to be short, medium or long term; and choosing if it is to generate an income or capital growth. That should help narrow the field slightly. Within that there can also be two approaches: the passive and analytical techniques.

Ethical investing

In addition to the criteria of timing, income, etc, there are other ways of picking an investment, such as by ethical or environmental standards for instance. There are two arguments that proponents advance for this approach: the first is that it is the right thing to do and everybody should do all they can to create a better world; and the second argument is that in any case the trend is for more people to care about such things, so as there is more widespread insistence on responsible and moral behaviour by companies both towards people and the earth, the companies with sound ethical policies are more likely to prosper. That means, they say, it is good not just for the conscience but the wallet. Critics of this approach point out that a strict application will eliminate many of the largest companies, which forces the investor onto smaller businesses which may have the potential for faster growth but also carry larger risks.

It is a matter of personal choice where to draw the line. Among classes of company shunned by some investors in recent years have been tobacco, armaments, makers of baby milk for Africa, oil, paper and timber (deforestation), mining, pharmaceuticals (animal testing), alcohol and so on, to say nothing of specific companies being boycotted because of their policies on pollution, ozone depletion, waste management, etc. Having a large number of strict criteria can cause confusion and rule out too many activities. For instance, an investor seriously opposed to gambling would presumably dislike the National Lottery, which could preclude all the shops and supermarkets that sell tickets. And how about buying gilts from a government that encourages arms manufacturers, trains soldiers and probably funds research centres that have animal experiments?

The ultimate point is that the investor should be able to sleep at night, not just because the money is safe, but also because there is no need to worry one is supporting a company that oppresses workers or helps to kill people. On the other hand it is then only fair that one not only avoids making a profit from the company's success but also stops buying its products.

Some unit trusts have been created to cater to such tastes, but not always with conspicuous investing success. That may also be true for an individual's portfolio. By excluding some large and possibly efficient companies the value of the investments as a whole may suffer. The point here is that one is investing not primarily for maximum return but for a decent income and decent morality by the companies.

A useful source of information on this is the Ethical Investment Research Service. It was set up in 1983 by several Quaker and Methodist charities and researches over 1,000 companies plus most collective funds and keeps a list of fund managers and stockbrokers concentrating on ethical investments. Another is Cantrade Investments (see Useful addresses at the end of this book). There is a separate stock market index for companies that meet a specified set of ethical criteria. It is called the FTSE4Good.

Risk/reward

One approach is to accept the efficient market hypothesis, or at least that a part-time investor who is an amateur in the market and lacks the resources or time to compete, is ill-equipped to out-guess the highly paid full-time professionals. This approach says the sensible course therefore is to pick the shares that provide a fair return for the degree of risk they involve. That just means one finds a number of ways of evaluating various risks and picks the best shares in various layers of risk.

There are two sorts of risk. One is connected with the company's management, business area and size. These may all indicate that it is more likely than most to suffer dangerous falls in profit or even to go bust. Though the casualty rate depends on the state of the economic cycle, quoted companies going belly up is not as rare an occurrence as one would imagine. The ones in danger will probably all have higher than average yields. This is called the equity risk premium, because it is generally recognized – not just in the stock market – that if you have to carry greater risk you should be rewarded with more money. Higher-risk companies with greater yield are fine for gamblers, or people with a sufficiently diversified portfolio to offset the risk by spreading across other less dangerous companies and sectors.

The second risk derives in part from a perception of this first risk. This is the tendency of some shares to react more violently to market movements. The degree of this responsiveness is known to professionals by the Greek letter beta – the share's beta is 1 when the price moves exactly in line with the return for the market as a whole (see Chapter 15). When it is greater than 1 it is called an aggressive stock, which moves by larger amounts than the market; this is a good one to have when the market is rising. Less than 1 moves less and is a good defensive stock at times of downturn. Shares with a high beta should provide a higher return on the investment as a compensation for the dangers.

That in summary is the passive approach, accepting the market's view and making the best of it to suit an individual's personal criteria.

Trackers

If the long and elaborate process of picking shares seems too hard, or even the risk/reward system seems daunting and it all requires more effort than you have to spare, you are not alone. Some of the sharpest minds in the UK and the United States have admitted the chances of being able consistently to pick the winners that outperform the market are pretty slim. And in any case, it may be just trying to gild the lily. The market as a whole, as represented by the FTSE 100 Index, does pretty well thank you on any reasonable timescale. As a result they produce 'tracker' funds, which track the main stock market index. They seldom buy all 100 shares in the FTSE 100 Index but they buy enough to drift along with it. That means that if it turns nasty you can at least say you are in good company. So the private investor can take a stake in one of these, or be a little more adventurous and go for an investment or unit trust with a broad but selective range of investments. See Chapter 6 for a description of exchange traded funds.

BUILDING A PORTFOLIO

Having a set of government privatization shares, grabbing at any promising mutualization and keeping a set of windfall shares, or accumulating random prospects, has the benefit of requiring no thought or planning. It is not very sensible though. The point of buying shares is presumably to make money, either by trading or by securing an income in time, perhaps for retirement. There are some guidelines for doing that.

Timing

When the mood for shares comes on you, do not rush into the market in a spending splurge. Wait until something genuinely promising comes along. It may take longer but at least it will ensure you do your homework seriously and do not just grab a company because some teenage scribbler in a newspaper thought it sounded good.

It will also help to think through not just what you buy, but the equally important factor of when (see Chapter 18).

Risk

Creating a balanced set of investments demands strategy as well as tactics. Assuming that on a risk continuum of 1 to 10 you are prepared to be cautiously brave by opting for 6, that does not mean every share has to be scored as a 6. It can mean a range of a really safe 2 with the occasional reckless flutter on something like an 8 or 9.

So each time a buying opportunity comes along, it is worth at least thinking about how it fits into the portfolio picture and how far it will move the overall average risk profile. This will have to be done more carefully the longer you hold shares, because as the prices move the various companies will change their percentage of the portfolio total and so their effect on the total risk balance also alters.

Losers

There is one outstanding characteristic shown by professionals that seems curiously absent in the casual amateur investor: the ability to cut losers. Small-time investors appear to have a sentimental attachment to shares they have bought, no matter how bombed out the company, or perhaps they just hate to admit mistakes which taking a loss would entail. The share price falls from 850p to 55p and they sit and wait for it to creep up again, though any dispassionate view will show it to be heading for something between 20p and hell.

Some investors even go in for 'averaging down' – buying more shares at the lower price to bring down the average cost of the stake. This is on the assumption the shares are about to recover. But you really do have to be absolutely copper-bottomed certain you are right and that the market will soon share your view to do that.

Probably more sensible is to see if there are better opportunities elsewhere in the market, and shed the loser. One way the big boys keep their policy in check and make such decisions easier and more automatic is by establishing an action point – the stop-loss signal is triggered by a fall of 10 to 15 per cent.

Winners

No company goes on soaring away for ever. Before getting too misty eyed at the success of a share that has doubled in price in the past three months, just stop and extrapolate – if it goes on like that will the company be able to buy the whole of France and Germany in five years' time? That creates a sense of perspective and may prompt one to cream off profits and distribute the proceeds to other likely successes.

One way to make such decisions easier is to set down action points at the time of purchase. You work out how much the share is undervalued – what would be its right market capitalization, price/earnings ratio, yield, or whatever, considering its sector, performance and prospects. When it passes that level on the way up you watch like a hawk for signs that the market realizes it has again overreacted, this time in the upwards direction, and you sell at least part of the holding.

A classic example was the boom in Internet-related shares in 1998 and 1999. Any business that had a new Web-based idea or that produced software for Internet trading, or invested in such enterprises suddenly became the philosopher's stone. Share prices doubled every six weeks and one went from 230p to £87 in less than a year; companies unknown a few months earlier were suddenly in the FTSE. It was heady stuff and many people were as carried away as they had been by previous such crazes, like the railways mania of the 1830s. The boom was clearly unsustainable and triggered an equally exaggerated reaction. It took over a year after that before more sensible approaches prevailed: the Internet is evidently a big business opportunity but will not inevitably provide limitless profits overnight. The sensible investors spotted the opportunities early, and the very sensible ones realized when the optimism had been overdone, and either sold or at least hugely reduced their holdings.

Random

If indecision gets too much there is always the dartboard system. The story is that one of the US business journals created a fund by throwing darts at the prices pages and it outperformed every one of the institutional funds over a period of three years.

SOURCES OF INFORMATION

Market signals

A warning sign is a company buying back its shares. It is an admission of management failure. It shows there are no more remunerative sources for the corporate cash in investing in the business. Or the business is trying to boost its earnings per share figure without changing the fundamentals.

Directors' dealings

Companies are obliged to tell the market about dealings in their shares by directors. This goes out on the stock exchange's news system and is occasionally picked up by an increasing number of newspapers.

Directors may provide very plausible reasons for selling, but it is best all the same to be wary and check what is going on. The director may really need the money for his children's education, to pay death duties or because he has just bought a small chateau in the Dordogne. But even then, why did he sell the shares of his own company to find the money? Without convincing explanations, one really does wonder what the managers of a business know that other shareholders do not when they start selling the shares in substantial quantities.

Conversely, the fact that several board members seem anxious to increase their holdings does seem pretty encouraging even if they are not acting on insider information.

Fashion

Fads overtake the world of investment with even greater virulence than women's clothing, and are equally evanescent. The experience with Internet shares is an example. At least that was related to some underlying business opportunity because it really was true the system was changing the way people do business, but nobody knew how much or how quickly, much less who was going to win during the trading revolution. As a result there was no obvious way of valuing an Internet company. Valuation was made additionally difficult by the variety: software producers, Internet service providers, retailers, etc. P/E ratios became insane or irrelevant (there were no earnings yet) and everyone knew the businesses were overvalued, but there seemed no way of stopping the boom. Until it stopped.

Unlike the Internet fashion, which at least derived from some confused perception of what really was going on, some fashions seem based on nothing but vaporous unrealistic hope. The point of which is twofold: it is not wrong to invest in a promising sector such as the Internet so long as you can see real value in the business, but is folly to get caught in the hysteria; and it is vital to separate the booms that are based on real business opportunities from the ones that are nothing but passing fads, apparently created by some sort of market ramp.

Sometimes a big takeover in a sector – banking, insurance, pharmaceuticals, retailing and so on – prompts speculation that others will follow and most of the shares in similar businesses suddenly romp ahead. Whether there is a sheep-like mentality in business, whether financial advisers then see the chance of income and urge their clients to grab a share of what is left, or whether managements really do fear being left behind, it quite often does in fact come true. It happened with demutualization of building societies and insurance companies. When one of those became a public company, owners of the others could not resist the lure of short-term profits and forced a flurry of yet others to follow.

When there is a general industry realignment of this type, the people who spot it at the start buy into the companies likely to become takeover targets and see healthy rises in the shares. Similarly carpetbaggers getting into the building societies in time emerge with a few thousand pounds of shares that they can swiftly extract.

Another fashion is for sectors. Suddenly biotechnology is seen as the saviour of mankind with untold riches to be derived from new drugs; or software companies are seen as the universal traders; or the Internet is thought to be a guaranteed means of selling to hundreds of millions of people at no cost at all; or a mining sector is reckoned to be certain to make a fortune from the spurt of demand for its metals. Vogues of this type seldom last more than a year, so it takes nimble minds to spot the trends, but the results can be spectacular. It is possible to increase the value of the holding by anything from five-fold to 20-fold in a matter of months. The point is to get out before the sky falls in.

Conversely, it is dangerous to climb aboard a bandwagon if it seems to have no real engine. If you do not understand what a company does or why it is valued as highly as it seems to be, avoid it.

Stockbrokers/investment advisers

If you have a stockbroker who is providing more than just a dealing service, or an investment adviser, there will be ample advice and information on tap. It may be very good advice, but intelligent investors are not wholly inert, prepared to accept everything they are told. You get better advice if you are informed enough to be able to discuss the market and your needs in an intelligent manner. So investors need to be continuously keeping up to date and to have their priorities clear. This is not just a useful antidote to being baffled by pretentious jargon; it also helps sort out whether one's ideas are right.

People without a regular financial adviser and those who distrust the advice they get have to hunt around for other sources. Stockbrokers' circulars are still generally available to them either directly or through the press, but usually after favoured clients have been told the conclusions and have had time to act on them. This is useful information because it gives a lot of background about a business, the calculations and feelings of a professional, and an indication of how the City may consider the shares. So you can then check what you feel, what the share price is doing and so on, and then use the additional insight as an extra aid in decision making.

Do not despair. Stockbrokers are as likely as anybody to be wrong. A classic case was the car-maker British Leyland. For about two years prior to its demise investors were getting more and more nervous about the unruly unions, the shoddy workmanship, the short-sighted management, and the increasing signs that the company could not make the cars the market wanted and was ill prepared to make the profound changes needed. So its shares slid steadily. Nevertheless, stockbrokers queued up throughout that inexorable tumble into insolvency to recommend the shares as a good buy.

Newspapers

All newspapers with any pretensions to seriousness have a City and investment section, and increasingly even the frivolous ones are responding to the demand for help. Both often reprint extracts from brokers' circulars, so one gets a feeling for what the professionals think. Do note, however, that brokers make money when investors buy or sell, but nothing if they hold on to their shares. Newspapers also report the results of a large number of companies and comment on a few of them. In addition, journalists meet people, look at results, talk to brokers and trade associations, and discuss business with independent commentators. In the course of this they may come across companies that justify a better rating and are currently being ignored by the market. They may therefore alert investors to shares that are undervalued, and by drawing attention to them may prompt an upward re-rating.

Tips like this can move a share, especially if it is in a tight market – there are not many free shares on issue. The rise is not purely because of buying, but also because market professionals read newspapers too, and so anticipate demand by moving up the prices. One consequence is that by the time you have read the buy recommendation, the price at which it was said to have been a bargain is sometimes just a memory.

It may still be worth acting on such buy recommendations, but you should bear in mind that newspapers are less good at spotting the shares that are due for a downward re-rating. It may be fear of the fierce defamation laws, or that journalists are just more geared to finding winners, but investors should not rely on newspapers for warnings of when to sell a share, which can be just as important a piece of advice. And nobody is much good at spotting in advance when the market as a whole is about to turn.

In addition to the daily and Sunday newspapers there are burgeoning specialist magazines. For what newspapers and magazines can tell you, see Chapter 12.

14 | What do you look for in company accounts?

Much of the analysis of suitable investments for both professionals and private investors starts with the company's annual report and accounts, and most of the ratios (see Chapter 15) are calculated from figures taken from the annual report. Most companies will be happy to forward a copy on request and large numbers of them are available on the Internet from Carol (see Useful addresses at the end of this book).

Annual reports and accounts amount to formidable documents apparently designed to ward off insomnia in all but the most dedicated, but you get nowt for nowt – investing your time before investing your money reduces the chances of doing something spectacularly silly. So it is worth learning a little of the meanings behind the figures, and the conventions used to prepare them. For a true understanding of a business one really needs to talk to production foremen, sales staff, van drivers, internal auditors and purchasing managers as well as the finance director to supplement the picture from the published figures and learn how the company fares. Unhappily this is not open to investors, though it would be for stockbrokers' analysts if they bothered to avail themselves of it.

The first rule to remember is not to be taken in by the spurious accuracy of having it all set down in precise-looking numbers. Everything in the annual report is the result of approximation, estimation, interpretation or guess. Accounting standards may limit the range of flexibility, but the company still has a pretty fair range of subjective assessment. That is in part because those rules themselves have to apply to a wide range of types and size of business and an enormous range of circumstances. As even the Accounting Standards Board conceded many years ago, corporate accounts can be relevant or comparable, but not both. It has in the main gone for relevance (the figures are tailored more to produce a fair picture of the business) at the expense of producing readily comparable accounts, which means investors get a better picture of the business itself but must put in some extra work to try and measure one business against another.

The second rule is that the purpose of accounts is to demonstrate that the business is being run honestly and the investors' cash is not being embezzled but is being well guarded. There is no intention to demonstrate competence, much less efficiency, though in a sophisticated secondary market that is what investors probably want. In the absence of direct hints about how clever the managers are, investors need to dig into the annual report to deduce suggestions from the available information.

It is partly to help that process that the accounting profession has for decades gone way beyond the demands of the Companies Acts in the amount of disclosure. The theory is that if all possible information is there, crooks and fools will have nowhere to hide. On the other hand, the UK is approaching the United States in the size of corporate documents and few can sift relevance from the mountain of figures. Some of it is unquestionably helpful in getting down to the details of how the numbers relate, but that usually acts as a substitute for finding out just what makes a business tick. The problem is being addressed by the Accounting Standards Board, which is suggesting three levels of accounts with varying degrees of detail, so that the private shareholder need be deluged with numbers only if they actually want to be.

A company's annual report and accounts may have plenty of material for the careful calculations of stockbrokers' analysts, but much of it will be incomprehensible, boring or irrelevant to most investors. Nevertheless the document does contain the occasional gems that indicate where the company is going and whether it is headed for riches or the knacker's yard.

Relying on the auditors too heavily is a mistake. They are accountants, nominally appointed by shareholders but in practice by directors, who are supposed to take an outsider's dispassionate view of the figures and to see that they have some relation to reality. Their main criteria are supposed to be derived from the requirement that the accounts represent a true and fair view, but increasingly they prefer the less contentious approach of saying the figures have been compiled in line with the rules. Even when they are conscientious, independent and rigorous, auditors are governed by the same uncertainties in the figures as the company itself. And in any case they cannot possibly check everything. As they themselves keep saying, they are guard-dogs, not bloodhounds – in other words they are there to check the figures add up and the stocks really are in the warehouse, but do not see their job as hunting through the business for signs of fraud or even incompetence. That is why auditors clearly say at the end of the report that it was the directors who prepared the accounts and who must take responsibility for them.

Such statements are also an attempt at a pre-emptive defence against litigation. When companies go under or are found to have been subject to massive fraud, creditors sue auditors because they have large professional indemnity insurance, rather than directors who may have carefully salted money away in overseas trusts or their spouses' names and therefore seem people of no substance. Directors are however responsible both in law and in fact for running the company, and shareholders should resist pressure to reduce their liability no matter how worthy the cause appears to be.

Another thing to remember is that accounts represent the past. They will not therefore necessarily give an accurate picture of where the company is now, much less where it will be in the future, especially in fast-moving trades or changing economies. Accounts are prepared on a 'going concern' basis, which means, among other things, that assets are valued not by how much they would fetch in a break-up but at their worth to the business.

None of this is intended to suggest that accounts are useless or misleading, merely that they need interpretation, are imprecise and represent the past. This means a little more work in trying to evaluate just what they really do suggest.

First, some conventions. Like the government, companies generally do not stick to the calendar year. Financial years start at any time, sometimes not even at the beginning of a month. There may be nothing sinister in this. Financial years start when the company was originally registered and it could be they have just stuck with it. Some businesses reckon their sales are seasonal and set the financial year so that the second half gets the benefit of the upturn.

Any number in brackets is a negative. So at the profit level of the accounts, £12.8 million indicates a profit but (£385,000) shows a loss. The numbers in the main pages of the accounts are mostly sums of various groups of numbers which are then shown in greater detail in the notes – there is normally a little number next to each line to show which note relates to it. It is also worth remembering that many of the numbers in the report are a bit barren on their own and have a far greater significance when related to other numbers in the accounts, set against previous years or in comparison with other businesses.

The main items in the document are the directors' report, the profit and loss account and the balance sheet. In addition there are the extensive notes, which are supposed to amplify or explain the figures, the source and application of funds that show where the company got its cash and how the money was used, and the auditors' report.

ANNUAL REPORT

Chairman's and directors' report

Right at the front there is usually a brief word from the chairman and the directors' report. These should say what the company does and sum up significant highlights of the year just completed, possibly with some comments on the performance and how the figures should be interpreted. There is often a word about prospects, which is only fair considering most reports are produced several months into the next financial year, but they seldom give more than a cursory suggestion. The usual formula is something like, 'despite the difficult financial circumstances we hope to continue developing the company and hope for further improvement in the results for the current year'. If the results turn out worse, shareholders cannot sue anybody for misrepresentation even on that small scale and, to be fair, even 3 months into a year may give a misleading picture of the results for the whole 12 months. One has therefore to learn to read between the lines and see what the phrases indicate and what the chairman is hinting at. Some also try to be as explicit as circumstances permit, and so do offer a veiled warning.

Accounting policies

Most of this is extremely boring and can safely be ignored as routine prescribed by the laws and accounting standards. Just occasionally, however, a company reckons the standard rules would produce nonsense and rather than mislead it intends to depart from the normal presentation. The report should explain what standard is being breached and why. The explanation of this may not always be the most lucid prose and is not primarily aimed at laymen, but a bit of careful attention will usually unravel it. If the auditors reckon it is a bit of flummery or a specious excuse they will comment on it in their report.

Profit and loss account

Turnover

The profit and loss account starts by showing the company's trading over the previous financial year. That shows turnover, which just means sales and sometimes is actually labelled so. Drinks companies sometimes then take off excise taxes to show net sales value. One can then see how this latest year compared with the previous one. Even if it looks healthy it is probably wise to flip to the note associated with the figure and see if there are breakdowns. Some companies show the sales by product, by geographical area, by market sector and so on. This will show whether there are any peculiarities, like one product supporting the sagging rest or one geographical area turning distinctly dodgy. If there is anything like that, turn to the chairman's and directors' reports to see if there is any explanation. The answer may be something simple like an acquisition or a disposal. If there is no explanation, such distortions or odd figures should prompt questions and trigger caution.

Operating profit

Next come the operating costs of running the company including everything from stationery to wages, which are often broken down into major components such as cost of manufacturing, distribution, administration, and research and development. These can sometimes suggest questions: why is administration so expensive, why has the company been cutting back on research for several years, and so on. When the cost of sales is deducted from the total turnover figure the result is the operating profit.

Other incomes

In larger companies you then get a variety of other incomes such as money paid to the parent company by subsidiaries, or occasionally the other way, and some exceptional items that are not a normal part of the company trading operations. A business has to pay interest on money it has borrowed. Any sharp movement in interest out or in that is out of line with prevailing interest rates should prompt searches in the notes and statements for explanations. It could be borrowings for acquisitions or for a large redundancy programme.

Pre-tax profit

When the operating costs and other incomes have been accounted for, what is left is the pre-tax profit, which is the figure normally used in newspaper accounts of results. Taking off corporation tax and dividend payments leaves the retained profit, which the business is planning to reinvest.

Accounting standards say exceptional items such as profit from the sale of an office building or the cost of a major reorganization and redundancy of many employees, have to be separated out.

Other items

The other items are fairly straightforward. The profit and loss table shows the amount being paid to shareholders in dividends, sometimes separating out preference shares. Anything left after that is transferred to reserves. This does not mean it goes into the company coffers; the term is confusing so some companies have opted instead to call the amount 'retained profits' or, to be even more explanatory, something like 'profits retained in the business'. This is the money that builds the company. It goes into buying machinery, factories, raw materials, or financing work in progress. Some companies have deprived themselves of this vital reinvestment because institutional shareholders demand a growing dividend cheque every year, even if that means starving the enterprise of cash – if the business suffers they will just ditch the shares and move on to another company.

There is nothing in the accounts that would suggest, for instance, a good start to the year but the whole business falling out of bed in its last three months and showing plunging sales and profits. All of that should be mentioned in the reports from the chairman and directors with explanations of why it happened and what they are doing about it.

A cliché is to talk about the bottom line, which is reckoned to come from accounts. In fact the bottom line of the profit and loss account, after the retained profits figure, is usually the earnings per share. Dividing the share price by this figure provides the P/E ratio or, to be precise, the historic P/E.

Balance sheet

While profit and loss accounts show an accumulation of transactions over the whole financial year, the balance sheet is a picture (traditionally called a 'snapshot' to emphasize how briefly relevant it is) of the financial position and assets on the last day of a company's financial year. Everything it owns or is owed, and everything it owes on that day is shown under a range of headings. By the time shareholders see the totals, the figures are largely irrelevant because in the intervening months everything could have changed.

The figures are, as with much else in the accounts, open to a degree of flexibility. For instance, valuations of assets are fairly subjective and depend on the purpose for which the figure is being prepared. A machine tool may be vital for the company but would fetch little if the liquidator had to break up the assets. Setting a price on patents, trademarks or brand names is even dodgier and there have been years of arguments about the true valuation of such intangible assets. The physical assets and stocks are often shown at cost, but inflation will have eroded that even if other factors have not altered the valuation. Similarly land values can move sharply with the vagaries of the economy and the property market.

What the accounts will show is the depreciation reducing the worth of assets. The notes and accounting policies usually elaborate on this, but machinery is normally written down by a fixed amount each year – straight-line depreciation. Clearly this leaves ample room for a bit of a nudge or window-dressing by adjusting valuations or bringing forward some items and delaying others, to give the figures the company wants to project. The snapshot may therefore be wholly atypical of the state of its finances on any other day of the year. Despite that it gives a hint of the financial health of the business, all the more so since the range of manipulations – short of outright fraud – is limited for a number of reasons, including accounting standards and the need to be reasonably consistent with the previous years.

In the list of things the company owns the first heading is fixed assets. This comprises things that have been and are likely to continue as long-term investments. So it includes things like factories and equipment, office blocks and the like. Lorries are also included under this heading, probably for want of a better place to put them. The value is normally in there at cost or what they would sell for, or some formula.

Then come investments in other companies. Then there are current assets, which covers the more mobile, changing things like stocks of raw materials and finished products in the warehouse, money owed by customers, and money in the bank.

After that comes a list of the company's debts. First there are current liabilities, or creditors expecting to be paid in under a year. This includes trade creditors (suppliers of goods and services who have not yet been paid), money borrowed short term, the money set aside for the proposed dividend, and the corporation tax to be paid on the profits. The total is then deducted from the current assets to show the net figure. This is sometimes called the company's working capital.

Longer-term debt includes things like a term-loan from the bank and provisions for known spending such as restructuring the business, moving the factory or the feared outcome of a legal case. Taking the short- and long-term liabilities from the assets produces the net asset figure.

Once again, there should be comparison not only with the previous year, which most companies provide, but also with the previous five years. Combining the current figure with previous years and knowing something about the norms in that industry should provide a pretty good measure of the company's financial health.

Cash-flow statement

A cash-flow, or flow of funds, or source and application of funds, statement is, as its names suggest, a supplementary indication of how the money flows in from profits and investments, and goes out again for tax, dividends and the like. In addition it gives the figures for repayment of capital – redeeming a debenture for instance – or finance in from raising further capital. There is little point in making a profit if the business just runs out of cash, and this is where the warning should show.

The final figure of the statement shows the growth or decrease in the company's funds during the year. That is a fairly good indication therefore of how successfully it has been managed.

Auditors' report

The auditors' report is normally a pretty routine affair, saying the company has abided by the accounting standards, Companies Act requirements and other rules; that the directors are responsible for the accounts; and the auditors merely take samples and tests as required by the Auditing Practices Board and that as far they can tell the accounts represent a true and fair account of the state of play. Just occasionally there is a qualified report.

In essence there are two sort of qualification, as a result of uncertainty or from disagreement with the way directors treat some item. The effect may be much the same but the message is signalled in different ways.

If the uncertainty is big enough to mention but not fundamental to the business, the auditors normally say, subject to the specific doubts that they will normally spell out, that the accounts are all right. That may just be the outcome of a court action and hence inherently uncertain, but it could also say the auditors could not tell if proper accounts had been kept in one part of the business.

Sometimes it is a straight disagreement about the treatment of an item. Once again, if it is a biggish number in the context of the accounts but not serious enough to undermine the company's survival, the auditors normally say it is all true and fair except for the specified item. The auditors may for instance say a debt in the balance sheet is not recoverable, for all the directors' optimism.

On a few rare occasions the split between the board and the auditors is so serious, or the auditors have stumbled on something so crucial to the company's viability, that a more serious warning is inserted into the accounts. If the doubts about record-keeping or the reliability of information generally are so great that the auditors have serious doubts about the whole thing, they will say they could not discover whether the stocks are present or the sales are as stated. The report may say the books and figures were not available, some tests of the books were frustrated, or there was some such deep problem about verifying what was going on, and as a result they can give no opinion on whether the accounts are true and fair.

Sometimes there is just a fundamental disagreement between the directors and auditors about what things are worth or how they should be treated. If these are such major items that they are fundamental to the state of the business, the auditors normally set out the problem – for instance the valuation of major long-term contracts – and say the accounts are as a result misleading. They normally add that had the accounting treatment been as they suggested, the profits would have been so many millions lower.

Such major rows are rare because the board and the auditors argue about such items at enormous length, and auditors would bend over backwards to avoid such open conflicts, if only because it is almost always the prelude to a change of auditor and the accountants losing a source of income.

Another worrying comment is that the accounts have been prepared on a going-concern basis, which enters the warning that the figures would be unjustified if the business went bust. Clearly that sort of point is not going to be made of a business with a booming present and a flourishing future.

Notes

Behind all these are the notes, frequently running to dozens of pages. It is a frightening and long set of technical-looking statistics. In fact this is where the real meat is generally buried.

A series of reports on corporate governance has produced the Combined Code, which the stock exchange backs and tells companies to include in their annual report, as it shows how far they complied with the requirements. In addition, some companies provide unaudited supplements giving breakdowns by product area and country of sales, sometimes by country of manufacture and other details.

This is the section where you will find how much directors earned and what sort of incentive and share-option packages they have. It will also show how many employees there are and how that total changed during the year.

Also at the back but not usually a formal part of the notes is a table showing previous years' performance, going back at least 5 and sometimes 10 years. This enables one to check whether sales have risen faster than the rate of inflation and whether the trend has been a steady one or erratic. It also tends to show the step change when the boost to profit and turnover came not from organic growth but an acquisition.

USING THE ACCOUNTS

This then is the start. Now these bare figures must be related to something to extract some meaning from them. For instance, the figure of the trade creditors as a percentage of turnover: the higher the percentage the longer customers are taking to pay. This means that not only must the company find expensive finance to bridge that gap, but also that its cash and credit control are not very good.

Another significant figure is the relationship between borrowings and share capital. Borrowed money has to be repaid and the interest is due whether the company is making a profit or not. Equity – share capital – is never likely to be repaid and dividends are paid only when the company can afford them. If the profitability is greater than the cost of debt, the profit attributable will be geared up substantially. All the same, there are limits on how much a company may borrow and borrowing makes a business vulnerable. The ratio between those borrowings and the equity money is called 'gearing' ('leverage' in the United States), and a company with shareholders' funds of £150 million and borrowings of £75 million would be called 50 per cent geared. It varies a bit depending on external circumstances and the industry sector, but if it went to over 60 per cent, the company would be called highly geared. (For further details of such ratios see Chapter 15.)

One aspect that is easy to study is the trends over time. All accounts provide the previous year's figures and many provide summary tables for the previous five years. These will show, for instance, whether turnover has risen faster than the rate of inflation, and whether profits have risen even faster through increased efficiency, concentration on high-margin products and so on.

OTHER INFORMATION FROM THE COMPANY

Interim reports

In between the annual reports companies also produce the results of trading in the first half of their financial year. These are generally pretty short documents giving a brief statement of the volume of trade and profit, plus an abbreviated balance sheet minus the copious notes. Some companies give some segmental information as well. The figures are not audited.

Prospectuses and listing particulars

Companies first coming to the stock market must provide extensive details not just about the business but also the people running it. Listing rules require all sorts of information about assets, depreciation, government grants, a brief history, auditors, bankers, financial advisers, stockbrokers, solicitors, a complete description of the business, details of management (directors are asking the government to be excused from putting in home addresses in future), staff and premises, what will be done with the money raised, expectations of the immediate future, and so on. So the prospectus is usually the most comprehensive information about itself that a company ever publishes.

Circulars on disposals and acquisitions

Shareholders must be told of any substantial acquisition, with details of the offer, why it is being made and how it is to be paid for. In most such cases the shareholders will have to ratify the board's decision to purchase.

Some bids are called 'hostile', though it is the business on the receiving end of an unwelcome offer that is belligerent. In such non-agreed takeover battles the 'target' will also send shareholders documents, defending its management, trading record and emphasizing its glowing future, as well as the need for continued independence. These tend to be accompanied by extensive disclosures, accounts and forecasts, rivalling the annual report in scope. Sometimes a higher offer seems to conquer such emphatic misgivings.

Newsletters

Shareholder loyalty has grown in importance in recent years, so companies try to keep their investors happy by sending them newsletters. Even more commonly, there are magazines and news-sheets distributed to employees, who sometimes also get a shortened version of the annual accounts. Careless companies sometimes tell a different story in house magazines and shareholder reports.

15 | Do the various ratios and formulae help?

Ratios and formulae provide the principal basis for fundamental analysis (see Chapter 13) – the methods for deciding what the underlying value of the company should be, and then deciding whether the market has got it right. (Some, like yield, net asset value, market capitalization, and price/earnings ratio are also covered in Chapter 12.)

Unfortunately there is no one simple and obvious way of deciding what a company is worth now, much less how its value is likely to move in the future. There are many ways of getting an indication and people have faith in different methods. What all the systems have in common is not being consistently and reliably able to paint a definitive picture of the business.

All the calculations are helpful some of the time; some most of the time. There are also fashions about which ratio is the most reliable indicator. One difficulty is that when one factor becomes generally applied as the true measure of a company there is a tendency to distort the whole picture. In other words, if dividend cover is taken as the true indication of a company's worth, businesses are ranked by that criterion and a sensible investor would do best to look harder at other factors to see if the market has got its evaluation right. Proponents of the efficient market hypothesis should believe the price sums it all up, but their actions belie such belief.

Many ratios are quite difficult to work out and need a bit of digging to get at the figures. Most of these figures are extracted from the company's annual report and accounts, so all this should be read in conjunction with the previous chapter on what to look for in those accounts.

All calculations and ratios show how intensively and effectively a company runs its business, but there are no absolute values for any of these items. That is because different industries have varying payment customs, there are inherent limitations on what can be put into stock, and so on. So the fairest way is to check what the norm is for the industry and see how far the company diverges from it. That in turn may take a fair amount of research from people like stockbrokers, trade associations and government.

The ones listed here are just the ratios in most common use and generally agreed to be helpful. Many experts have a wide range of other calculations, indicators and ratios they find useful. They can be handy, but only long experience will show what indicators are personally useful, so it will be the more experienced investors who should investigate the serious textbooks on how to calculate and use more sophisticated models of stock-market behaviour.

Acid test

Sometimes called the 'quick ratio', this can be worked out from the balance sheet. This is a slightly better version of the net current asset and current ratio (see below) because it assumes that not all current assets are equally available to be turned into cash if suddenly needed. For instance, stock and work in progress need time to realize or they will fetch very low prices, and in any case few companies would plan to liquidate all their stock just to pay an overdue bill. So the acid test is reckoned a more realistic measure of how easily a company could meet its bills.

It checks to see just how solvent a company is by having a look at its liquid or readily realizable assets that could be used to meet short-term liabilities, and then comparing these with its current creditor position. This means dividing the current assets minus stocks (ie, net monetary assets) by the current liabilities.

If the result is less than 1 it could not settle all immediate debts if they were called. One means a precarious balance and 2 is safer.

It is also worth checking back in previous accounts to see if there is much movement.

Asset backing

See net asset value.

Average collection period

Allowing customers credit is expensive because it ties up a company's own capital until the bill has been paid. So it is a mark of good management that debts are collected promptly. One method is to check the average collection time in days. It is calculated by dividing the trade debtors by total sales and multiplying the result by 365.

Beta

This is one of the few calculations in this chapter not derived from a company's accounts. It is a measure of the share price volatility relative to the rest of the stock market – which is a measure of risk, or at least of getting one's money out when needed. So beta measures how far an individual share moves compared with the market as a whole.

The market is taken to have a beta of 1, so a share with a beta of 1 moves exactly in line with the market as a whole. A beta of 1.6 would move 16 per cent when the market as a whole moves 10 per cent. A high positive beta indicates that the share can be expected to rise faster than average in good times but plunge more steeply in bad. This is characteristic of smaller companies.

Conversely, a share with a beta of less than 1 such as 0.8 rises and falls less than the market as a whole. A share with a negative beta (pretty rare) should move in the opposite direction to the other shares.

Current ratio

A way of looking at a company's ability to pay bills in the short term is to look at the cash it has and the things that can readily be turned into cash. It is arrived at by dividing current assets by current liabilities. If the result is 1 the two are identical and the company has no spare money. A reassuring figure is more like 1½ or 2 at least.

On the other hand, a high figure suggests the company may have an unusually large amount of stocks, or that it is keeping its assets in cash, which means it earns a larger return on lending than on the business itself or that it cannot find a suitable way of growing its real activity. All are potentially worrying and might suggest the company could make an attractive takeover target for someone in search of cheap cash. It is worth checking, however, whether the figure is representative of the industry.

Debt collection

This is also called 'debtor turnover' because it measures the number of times debtors are turned over in the year, which is a pretty good measure of how efficient the company is in shaking the money out of customers. The calculation is very simple: just divide the figure for sales by the end-year figure for the amount of debt.

Debt/equity ratio

See Gearing.

Dividend cover

This is the name given to the comparison between earnings per share and dividends. It shows what portion of the company's earnings is being paid to shareholders. So if Windowledge plc paid a dividend of 4p a share and its earnings per share were 12p, its dividend would be covered three times. That would be reckoned to be pretty conservative. Dividends at least twice covered are reckoned all right, but if the cover is only 1½ it is becoming worrying. At 1, all the earnings are distributed to shareholders and if it drops to below 1 the company is paying out retained profits from previous years. A low level of cover combined with high yield shows the market is nervous about the company's ability to go on paying at this rate. Different industries have different needs for cash, so comparisons should be made within the sector.

Dividend yield

This is the amount of dividend per share (usually quoted net of tax) as a percentage of the share price. It gives the return on the investment at the current share price and current rate of payments by the company. As with price/earnings ratios the calculation can be done on 'historic' figures, which would be based on the most recent dividend figure, or prospective, which would use the forecasts of what the next dividend is likely to be. So if Windowledge paid a dividend of 4p, and its share price is 390p the yield is only a pretty meagre 1 per cent.

That is pretty low in absolute terms, but one needs also to compare it with the yields on other shares in the sector to get the full flavour. As with price/earnings ratios (see below) comparison with competitors gives a good indication of the way a company is regarded by the market. Yield is determined by share price, so if a company's yield is below that of competitors, it seems investors expect quite a lot of improvement in the years ahead to bump up that figure.

Conversely, if a yield seems temptingly high and the share price is low, perhaps it is because there is a feeling that the company is heading into trouble and may well cut its dividend, at the very least. Once again, it will take further detective work to see how reasonable those expectations are.

Employee efficiency

This is calculated by dividing wages by sales times 100, to get a proportion of sales paid out in employee costs. This figure needs very much to be related to the sector since it is obviously nonsense to compare capital-intensive with labour-intensive businesses.

Gearing

The ratio between a company's borrowed money and the money that has been put in by shareholders (which is also known as equity) is called 'gearing' ('leverage' in the United States). So a high level of gearing – lots of borrowing in relation to the equity – exposes a company in a downturn and is therefore a high-risk strategy. Correspondingly shareholders of highly geared companies do rather well during upturns.

High short-term borrowing leaves a company vulnerable, especially during lean periods. If interest rates rise, the business can face a sudden and disastrous drain on its resources. If the company failed to maintain sufficient funds to cover interest, creditors could demand their cash and, failing to get it, could cause the company to be broken up. Banks can call in overdrafts at will and at times of economic downturn get twitchy enough to do so even at the cost of killing the business. Interest has to be paid on borrowed money whether the company can spare it or not, and the capital must at some stage be repaid. Shares do not have this problem. If times are tough the company can 'pass' (not pay) a dividend payment with impunity. Its share price may suffer but at least the business does not fold.

Some borrowing is pretty well inevitable and indeed if the return on the overdraft money is greater than the cost, the company and its shareholders benefit. Borrowing is also a more tax-efficient way of raising capital than issuing shares. The question is not how much has it borrowed but how great are those loans in relation to the value of the business. Bankers are also happier if the portion of borrowing is low because it shows that the borrowers – the owners of the company – are prepared to hazard their own cash.

There are various ways of working out the figures. The simplest is just to take the total borrowings and compare that figure with the total amount of shareholders' funds. That is also the crudest way of evaluating the business. You can refine the calculation of just how great the risk is (gearing is a way of measuring risk) by leaving out the less significant components. For instance, you can exclude short-term debts since these are just the day-to-day business procedures as opposed to the underlying indebtedness. On the other side, some people prefer to leave out intangible assets (such as trademarks) as difficult to dispose of, and sometimes preference shares are excluded from the total of shareholders' funds.

Net asset value

One way of judging a company is by the fail-safe system of seeing what it would be worth if the worst came to the worst and it went bust. The only real way is to check the value of all the assets it owns. In practice if the company did go under and had to sell everything it had, the assets would probably not realize the book value because fire sales seldom get best prices.

The figure, often abbreviated in newspapers and elsewhere to NAV, can be calculated from the balance sheet by adding up the book value of all a company's assets (including buildings, machinery, cash at the bank, investments, etc). Deduct from that all the liabilities (such as unpaid bills, borrowings, etc) as well as all capital charges such as debentures, loan stocks and preference shares. The remainder is the shareholders' equity in the company, or the net worth of the business. Divide this figure by the number of ordinary shares on issue to get the net asset value per share.

The result provides a direct measure of investment trusts because it can be compared precisely with the share price to see whether the trust stands at a discount or premium. In an industrial business, allowing for the fact that the book value of assets is not always what they would fetch in the open market, the result is an indication of just how much solid worth lies behind each share. It is not so much what you have as what you do with it, so the figure is generally only another factor to remember rather than a guide for investment. A company with net assets 20 per cent higher than the share price would make a tempting take-over target. If an offer does come, shareholders can then use this measure as one test of how fair the offer price is.

Net current assets

The calculations so far have been based on total net assets. Some people use a narrower measure – net current assets, which concentrates on cash, things that can readily be turned into cash and money owed that is likely to be paid in under a year. Net current assets per share being well above the share price intensifies the attractiveness of the business to a takeover predator. There is profit with a minimum concern or doubt because the business can be sold off in bits without worrying whether long-term assets are worth their book value. So the shares are worth buying because either somebody is going to make the assets work harder – new management or an outside buyer – or it will go bust, in which case there will be more than enough to pay off creditors and still have money left over to pay shareholders.

Subtracting a company's current liabilities (its debts and unpaid bills) from the current assets, both of which figures are available from the accounts, gives an idea of solvency in the short run.

If there is a big surplus the company has lots of spare cash or near-cash to pay debts in the coming year and could therefore get quite a lot of additional credit if needed. A figure close to nothing or, worse still, a deficit, is cause for alarm. See also Current ratio.

Price/earnings ratio

P/E is the most commonly used investment ratio; it so widely accepted that it is even printed in the newspaper share price columns (see Chapter 12). In effect, this is a measure of how quickly the market thinks the company will grow over the next year or two.

To get the figure, divide the share price by the company's earnings per share. For example, if Windowledge Holdings International has issued 70 million shares and made a profit of £8.4 million, then its earnings per share would be 8,400,000/70,000,000, which is 12p. (In practice calculations are a little more complex since earnings can be defined in different ways.) If the share price is 390p, then the price/earnings ratio is 390/12, which makes it 32.5. In effect that means it would take 32½ years of earnings at the current level to pay for the current share price. That is so long a period; however, there is obviously something else going on. What is creating such an unrealistic figure is the expectation by investors that the company will not be making the current level of earnings but is likely to grow fairly rapidly. As a result, the time taken to cover the current share price is likely to be a lot less than those 32½ years.

A relatively high P/E therefore indicates the presumption of fast growth. The point is the word 'relatively'. At one level it is a comparison with the market as a whole, and at another level it is with other companies in its sector. To get the full flavour of what the P/E indicates one has to take a look at the FTSE All Share Index P/E, as well as the same ratio for the sector in which the company operates (such as utilities, distribution, leisure). That indicates how the company compares, and the ratio is most useful as a relative risk indicator.

Even then the actual P/E ratio is not a final answer. The P/E discloses what the stock market as whole thinks of the prospects for the company. The work then starts to dig out some reason why it is at that level – why the market takes that view. If the P/E is high relative to its sector, is that because the company is fashionable (journalists all keep saying how wonderful the managers are), or is it because it really is about to grow at twice the rate of other comparable companies? The figure may be prompted by something simple like the rumour of an impending bid for the company, or there is some other obscure reason for the shares being unrealistically overvalued.

Conversely a low P/E indicates pessimism or lack of interest by other investors. Whether that gloomy view is justified and whether subsequent events will reverse it requires quite a lot of further thought. The P/E being higher or lower than the sector average merely tells you what others think, not whether they are right in their forecasts.

The historic P/E is calculated on the basis of the last published accounts, or prospective in which case they are based on forecasts of the next set of figures.

Profit margin

To find the underlying profitability of a company's trading, take trading or operating profit as a percentage of turnover. This is called the 'profit margin'. The figures will vary enormously between trades.

Quick ratio

See Acid test.

Return on capital employed

The point of a company is to make a surplus, its profit. The reason it borrows money or sells shares is to increase that profit. So an important gauge of its success is to see just how well it does that. The return on capital employed measures the efficiency with which the company is using its long-term cash.

To get this measure, one divides the trading profit (before exceptional items, interest and tax) by the average capital employed over the period (shareholders' funds plus borrowings) and multiplies the result by 100. A return of 10 per cent is the bare minimum required; 20 per cent is pretty good. A low return on capital shows inefficiency in the way the company is using the cash, even if the profit margins are high. The first check is to see whether the percentage is higher than the cost of borrowing. It is instructive to compare the return on cash in the business with other things the company (or indeed its investors) might have done with it.

A common criterion is to see what it would have yielded if put into something really safe, like gilts. If the return from that sort of investment is at least as great as the company's, there is something wrong – there should be a 'risk premium' for putting the money into something more hazardous such as a business venture. If the yield from gilts is at least 5 per cent lower than the return from the company's use of the money, the investment is beginning to seem reasonable. Investors prefer something better than 7 or 8 per cent above the gilt yield.

Return on sales

This is a revealing figure because it gives an indication of profit margins. Start with the pre-tax profit before interest and extraordinary items, then divide that figure by total sales, and multiply the result by 100.

Return per employee

This is another measure of how efficiently a business uses its workers. It is calculated by dividing the operating profit by the number of employees.

Return to shareholders

This is another measure that is not derived from the published accounts. It indicates the total performance of an equity over a period such as a year. The figures come from adding the change in share price (ie, price at the end of the period minus price at the start), plus the dividends, plus the interest receivable on the dividends, and then expressing this as a percentage of the price at the start of the period being examined.

For example, a share started the year at 520p and finished the year at 670p. During the year the company paid a 40p dividend as the interim dividend and 50p as the final. The interest rate was about 6 per cent. That would mean the share price benefit was £1.50 and the total dividend was 90p. Interest earned by putting the interim dividend money to work is 1.2p and the assumption is there has not been time to earn interest on the final. So the gain equals £1.50 + 90p + 1.2p = 241.2p, which divided by the 520p opening price is 0.46, so the return is slightly over 46 per cent. Not bad, but it is only a notional profit since it would entail selling the shares to realize it, and there would be a fee to be paid, which would reduce the benefit.

Stock turnover

Divide the cost of sales by the stock level at the end of the year.

Value added

This notion was developed in the 1990s to measure how a business has increased the value of the shareholders' investment.

Yield

See Dividend yield.

16 | Whose advice can you trust?

At the simplest level, nobody's; even at the broadest outline level. Nathan Rothschild said, 'The way to make money on the Exchange is to sell too soon.' Another member of the banking family, Solomon Rothschild, trading in the first half of the 19th century, agreed: 'One must get into the market as into a cold bath – quick in and quick out.' Timothy Bancroft, on the other hand said, 'Buy good securities. Put them away. Forget them.'

Then there are the books of advice on how to go about it. Waterstone's bookshop in London's Piccadilly has 66 feet of shelving filled with books advising people on how to pick a share, how to beat the market, how to be cleverer than stockbrokers, how the successful investors have done it, what the mathematical formulae are for deciding when and what to buy. All with apparently infallible ways of making the reader a major fortune.

How about on individual shares though? Think of it this way – what sort of philanthropy could it be that persuades some nice person to make you rich instead of himself? If journalists really knew which share to buy and when, would they still be hacking away at the computer instead of lolling on some Caribbean beach? How can the authors of books like *Make a Killing on the Stock Exchange, How to Pick the Winners, Selecting the Soaring Shares,* and so on afford to spend all those hours writing when they should be too busy becoming billionaires by trading? Indeed, if they were good, why would they share the secret when your buying might inflate the shares they would have wanted to buy?

All advice should be treated with scepticism. Even this. There used to be an old stock exchange maxim: 'Where there is a tip there is a tap.' What that meant was that if somebody is persuading you to buy a share there is probably some self-interested motive such as that somebody having large amounts of that company's shares on tap waiting to be sold when the price rises.

This is not a nihilist view, and does not mean disregarding all sources of information, just recognizing that nobody is always right, and the decision lies in the investor's own mind. No excuses, no defences, no attempts at shuffling off the blame: you choose.

There is no shortage of help and advice around and much of it is jolly useful, but even while extracting the practical bits one needs, none of it should be regarded as holy writ. The broadsheet newspapers, for instance, have not only share prices pages, but also carry company news and analysis columns that look at the latest results of large companies. Many of the Sunday papers also sometimes reprint the buy and sell advice of stockbrokers.

In keeping with the scepticism, one should ask about the expertise of stockbrokers. First, they have an incentive to persuade everybody to be active traders and therefore continuously to adjust their portfolios, to buy and sell shares, because they make money from deal commissions only if people are trading – it does not matter which way – while if people sit on their holdings, the brokers starve. Second, most of their analysts are clever graduates but few have ever got their fingernails dirty in industry, so although they understand all the corporate ratios, meet the chairmen and finance directors, and sometimes even visit factories, they have little feel for commerce. But with that proviso their advice is extremely helpful because what they do understand is the stock market. So they have a much better feel than the lay investor for how the City, including institutional investors, will react to a company and its performance. Since these are the people who influence share prices, this information is invaluable.

Stockbrokers issue circulars on companies, having plodded through the annual report. The average small investor generally does not have access to these circulars, and would probably have little use for them if he or she did. By the time they are printed the professionals have already acted on any insight in them, and there is little evidence that stockbrokers are markedly better prophets than the rest of us. It is not a matter of saying, if you are so clever why are you not rich (because many of them are pretty comfortably off), but would they still be working for wages if they could make amazing fortunes by merely investing?

At least the better newspapers and magazines, unlike stockbrokers' analysts, assess the performance of their share tips at the end of the year. If they do not, you can be pretty sure performance has been dismal. Even that is not a guide though, because personnel change.

The newspapers themselves are now on the Web (eg www.ft.com, www.telegraph.co.uk), so one can check back through the archives to see what they said about a company or the state of the economy. Other online sites worth exploring are Home & Finance (www.fmlx.com) for investment tools; the publishers of the Company Guide and REFS (www.hemscott.co.uk); and www.news-review.co.uk for a summary of useful news and information.

So, there is lots of advice about, but little of it is disinterested and what there is is not always right. So listen to as many sources of advice as you can, weigh them against common sense and use them as a factor but not as the final arbiters of an investment decision. This is made even more important by remembering their criteria may be different. As Shaw said, do not do unto others as you would have them do unto you; their tastes may not be the same. So, no matter how careful and accurate the advice, it may stem from different priorities and preferences.

This is not a counsel of despair, merely of wariness. While everybody's information and advice should be treated with care, there are many sources of information that may not in themselves be the deciding point but will contribute to the proper thinking about what and when to buy.

17 | Can you recognize high-risk shares?

There is no such thing as a risk-free investment. Come to that, there is no risk-free life. There is capital risk, company risk, exchange rate risk, income risk, inflation risk, market risk, sector or industry risk and so on. When deciding on investments this is precisely one of the earliest questions in narrowing the field – just how much risk is acceptable? In this context that usually means capital risk – ie the danger that the share price falls or, worse still, that the company founders.

That can happen because a business is badly run, its managing director is killed in a car crash, the two biggest customers are nationalized or go bust, and so on. It can also be because the business sector is doing badly through a change in fashion or competing products arriving, health dangers associated with the product, etc. It can also be because the whole market has fallen flat on its face. Or the results can be hit by dangers in the currency market or interest rates.

There are ways for an investor to gauge risk in advance. The first and most obvious way is to look at the business that a company is in. Some trades have been shown by history to be dodgy or at least volatile, and some we can tell from instinct are vulnerable. They may move sharply with fashions, season or the economic cycle.

The second way to judge is to look at the management. This is not open to everybody, except in a few cases. For instance, consumers know from personal experience that there are some goods, some shops and some service companies that really seem good value, and this keeps them buying. Other consumers may well feel the same way, in which case it could be a good business. And of course the opposite is equally a warning – if you have stopped buying some goods or going to a chain of shops because the goods are shoddy or the value is poor, sooner or later others are likely to spot that as well.

Then there are available company financial figures. These come in the accounts and are filed at Companies House. Extracting information from the mass of data in published accounts is a painstaking business requiring application and experience, though reading Chapter 14 will help. There is nothing difficult about it, but one has to learn the language of accounting, have an inkling about some of the dodges companies use (see *Accounting for Growth*, by Terry Smith) and understand the significance of the numbers.

Another good indicator is the way the rest of the world regards the business. There are three useful indications of this: the beta, the price/earnings ratio and the dividend yield (see Chapter 15), the last two of which are available on the newspaper share prices pages. Beta is a measure of the price volatility, measured against the market as a whole and is strongly correlated with risk. The P/E is the price of the share divided by the attributable earnings. Thus a high P/E says that the market expects a faster than average growth, and a low one means there is a general feeling that the company will languish. In effect the price reflects, or discounts, the expected growth in the dividends the company will pay over the next few years. A very low P/E by contrast indicates a lack of enthusiasm in the market, probably because it considers the business risky.

The yield will show a similar pattern. There is a caveat here, though. Some shares have a low P/E and a high yield not because they are intrinsically dodgy but because they are unfashionable. And this is where the so-called perfect market breaks down and a shrewd investor can get an edge on the professionals. For instance, companies with a small market value were avoided for years for two main reasons: first, the major investment funds could not fit them into a policy of buying in big chunks of money yet ending up owning only a small percentage of a company;

second, few analysts bother to look at most of the shares. This neglect meant it was possible for the small investor to find relatively high yields on investments by buying these companies' shares.

Similarly, if a couple of major companies in a sector – retailing, computers, insurance or whatever – report lower profits, leaner margins and tough times ahead, all the similar companies will be marked down. There is some sense in that since the chances are most of them will be affected in a similar way. If one discovers, however, that by good luck, good management, or good products, one company in the disdained sector actually has cash in the bank and is achieving a substantially higher profit margin than most of its competitors (and the figures are reliable and not just window-dressing), then that company will provide a relatively cheap way in, either for good income or for capital growth when market sentiment reassesses the whole area of business. In other words, the signals of high risk were misleading or mistaken.

It is a foolhardy investor who relies heavily on this sort of luck or imagines he or she knows better than the market. In general the market is more often right than wrong and the figures really provide a pretty good indication that there is something potentially dodgy. It is sometimes possible to find gold where others see only dross, but do not rely on it.

With investments as with the rest of life: there are no free rides. Everything has a price. If something has a higher risk it is likely to offset that with a higher return. What victims always forget when they get caught in something like the Bank of Credit & Commerce International or Lloyd's, or a series of frauds like the Nigerian scam or the prime bank paper, is that the corollary of that rule also applies: if there is a higher than expected return there is probably also greater danger. Only very small children and people whose greed overcomes their common sense expect something for nothing in this world.

There is, however, a market in risk. One can hedge against it – take financial measures to limit the extent of the risk. Companies hedge their currency exchange exposure on foreign trading by buying currencies forward and other such devices. An investor can limit losses on a share by buying options.

The most important aspect is to take a reasoned approach:

▌ be aware that there are risks involved in all investments;
▌ decide how much risk you are prepared to accept;
▌ realize no one share can match the preferences;
▌ balance the spread of shares to match risk needs;
▌ assess each new investment to maintain the balance.

18 | When do you buy shares?

The obvious answer is, when they are cheap. Predictably, there are a few problems to that, including deciding how you define cheap, finding the stock that is cheap and deciding just why it is cheap. So important is this aspect that experienced investors will tell you it is more important to judge when to buy than what to buy.

One of the problems with the stock market is the herd instinct that drives it hither and yon on superstition, greed, fashion and uncertainty. So when the market is rising everybody piles in because they fear being left out when the profits are being made. It is not that they are ignorant of the fundamental principle behind making profits – buy cheap and sell dear – they just happen to think that even at a time of high prices (judged by yield, price/earnings ratios, or the yield gap) the shares are cheap because they will probably go far higher.

In the reverse phase, investors both private and institutional sell shares that on most criteria would be reckoned cheap because they expect them to go on plunging further.

In 1710 to 1720 a series of 'bubble' companies burst onto the stock market, of which the South Sea Company (actually the full and splendidly rolling name of the enterprise was The Governor and Company of Merchants of Great Britain Trading to the South Seas and Other Parts of America and for Encouraging Fishery) was merely the most notorious. Its shares were issued at £100 and started 1720 at £128 10s 0d. By August they had reached £1,050 but finished the year back at £124 before the company collapsed.

In the 1830s it was railway mania, with any company even vaguely connected to trains being relentlessly pursued by investors wanting to put yet more money into it. More recently we have had other enthusiasms. At one time being in computers was all the rage and anything to do with electronics saw its shares knock the roof off. Later the enthusiasm moved on to biotechnology when everybody expected miracle drugs, 'silver bullets' and panaceas from the science. Then the Internet grabbed the imagination to produce eye-watering share price rises. There are people who spot these trends at the early stages before enthusiasm reaches the level of hysteria, and some also spot the stage when expectations have reached wholly unrealistic levels that cannot long be sustained and so get out.

You can recognize a bull market reaching its peak by the unanimity of opinion that happy days are here again. Even the tabloids start talking about the stock market: there are pictures everywhere of champagne-swilling young dealers, serious economists saying this time it is different, people who would not normally know a balance sheet from a bed sheet starting to buy shares, and the shares themselves are on absurdly high price/earnings ratios and low yields.

The downturn happens in one of two ways. There is either a sudden trigger like a huge and swift hike in the price of oil or there is just a lassitude when nothing seems quite right. The shares fail to respond to good news, but relapse at every sign of adverse news. That is when to stop buying, at the very least (see Chapter 26).

At downturns, institutions and private investors prepare for the end of capitalism as we know it. To be fair there is also in part a rational reason for all this: during booms people have higher disposable income both for direct investment and for pensions and insurance (with those companies then channelling part of the cash into the market), while during a recession there is unemployment, negative equity and an absence of pay rises.

At the simplest level much of the investor's aim can be achieved by being just counter-cyclical: see which way the herd goes and head the other way. On the other hand it takes strong nerves to buy in a bear market when gloom and despondency suggest shares will plunge further and companies by the score will topple over. It also takes stern self-discipline to take profits in a roaring bull market, knowing that shares may well rise further and one is therefore foregoing some of the extra profit. Even in this apparently simple strategy, however, timing is all.

_____

When the market has been sliding for some time the careful investor will start to check whether the bottom can be in sight. It takes courage and strong nerves. For a start you have to face the fact that you are very unlikely to buy at the absolute bottom and sell at the very top. If you do in fact manage either, never mind both, admit it to be pure fluke. So there are two possible timings: when it (the market, the sector, the individual share) is still heading down but one has a reasonable feeling there cannot be much further to go; and when prices have just tentatively started coming off the bottom. Get the timing wrong and the prices will continue to tumble, and it takes a hardy soul with a gambler's instinct to go in for 'pound cost averaging' at that stage – putting the same amount in again as the price falls to get even more shares.

A sign that the market is pretty well at the bottom is when the share prices have already been discounted for doomsday. On the one hand, they have allowed for more massive slumps than it is rational to expect. In fact the share prices have anticipated so much bad news that they no longer react to it when it comes. On the other hand, the price does start to stir and rise a bit when even the slightest glimmer of good news comes along. That is the time to start hunting for good value.

That sort of thinking applies to the market as a whole and also to individual shares. A very successful large company into which everyone has put their pension money for years, suddenly stumbles. It makes a few mistakes, loses some orders, miscalculates the market or whatever, and issues a profit warning. The disillusion hits the professionals so badly that they abandon the fallen star in droves. Though small companies die in dozens and the occasional middle-ranking company succumbs, it is fairly rare for a major commercial undertaking to go belly up. There have been the Leylands, Polly Pecks and the like over the years, but that is still pretty unusual. Even if the board cannot immediately retrieve its mistakes, bring in new managers or just get back on its old track, there is a good chance somebody will be waiting to snap up the business in a takeover.

Like all other contrary views it takes caution and care. The people who specialize in this sort of investment normally wait until the first and second tumbles have worked through the market and the share price is bumping along a steady low, before starting to buy.

There are two sets of timings to consider. One concerns the market as whole, and the second is for the individual share that has already been identified (see Chapter 13 on picking shares). Among the factors affecting the market as whole are:

▋ the general economic cycle (and that could be anything from a recovery to a slowing in anticipation of a recession);
▋ the level of inflation;
▋ interest rates, since they affect consumer demand as well as the costs of business and hence profitability;
▋ tax levels and the changes;
▋ the relative strength of the currency, since that affects the cost of imports and the competitiveness of exporters;
▋ the political situation, including the proximity of elections and who is likely to win.

On top of that are the external influences. For instance, the London stock market reacts in sympathy with US stock markets: the main market moves in reaction to the Dow, and technical stocks are influenced by the movements of the Nasdaq. This provides the background for looking at and trying to extract information from recent price movements, and sets the context for examining individual companies.

Everyone has heard of bull markets when everything is booming and prosperity will never end, and bear markets when prices plunge and the economy and people are in deep depression with no visible hope of salvation. Back at the end of the 19th century Charles H Dow, who helped start the Dow Jones Index for the Wall Street Stock Exchange as well as found the *Wall Street Journal*, detected a pattern in share price movements. He reckoned these followed a regular enough progression to be able to forecast where the price will go next.

The Dow Theory says there are great long-term patterns, called primary trends, which create the bull or bear markets that can dominate an economy for several years. Within these are shorter-term fluctuations that go against the overall trend, reinforce it, or predict its turn, and these he called secondary reactions. Finally, there are the daily oscillations that are called, predictably enough, tertiary patterns.

The accountant Ralph Elliott worked on a larger scale. He talked of grand super-cycles lasting 150 to 200 years within which there are shorter fluctuations. There are many books on such topics but they are probably a touch specialized for an amateur investor.

Within these grand economic cycles are price movements of the market and of individual shares, and if the trend or pattern can be spotted in time there is an opportunity for profit. This is the province of the technical analyst who relies principally on charts of market changes. At the most bloodthirsty these people assert it is not necessary to know even the name of the underlying instrument, whether it is a share, a currency, or a commodity, because everything is in the price. More particularly, the price is set by market psychology and since human behaviour is fairly constant, the pattern can be extrapolated. The trick is therefore to detect patterns in time and then act on them. That requires charts, usually of price movements.

Charts represent one of the two main ways of assessing a share. The other is fundamental analysis. That is a thorough study of the company and its accounts, the markets in which it operates, and the quality of its management (see Chapter 13 for how to pick a share).

The aim of all these is to reinforce other criteria for choosing a share or a time for buying, and not to use them in isolation. That applies also to different types of chart. Checking to see how the price of a company's share moves in relation to the market as a whole is sometimes an indication to help with the decisions. Shares with a wildly fluctuating relative strength are likely to be unpredictable performers and so a more risky investment. On the other hand, if the company has for some time been sagging, with the shares consistently underperforming the market as a whole, and its relative strength starts improving, this might reinforce the decision to buy that was prompted by other signals.

Charts may be better at giving added information about individual shares than about the market as a whole.

William D Gann, a mathematician and successful trader in shares and commodities, produced a variant of this concentrating more on support and resistance levels and the speed of price change, but the explanation is well nigh incomprehensible to anyone with less mathematical expertise.

The patterns can be explained by psychological descriptions of the way people behave, and these seem quite plausible – but not to the academics who have used mathematical analysis to produce the 'random walk' theory. This says the prices move totally unpredictably and charting the tossing of a coin would produce similar patterns. In addition, the 'efficient market' hypothesis says information is so swiftly and uniformly disseminated that nobody can get an advantage to outperform the market. That, however, ignores the time factor, and the obvious fact that some people do very nicely indeed, thank you.

It is not quite as straightforward as a brief explanation makes it sound. Even if the random walk theory and efficient market hypothesis are dismissed as being not universally applicable, there are problems with charts. For a start they require expert interpretation of shapes that are seldom as simple and obvious as the illustrations in books. Just when does a fluctuation indicate a turn and when is it merely a temporary correction? Even with other financial knowledge to test the plausibility of an indicator, and even with extensive experience of interpreting charts, the chances of making mistakes are high. That means a fallible subjective judgement about a developing pattern, and some people are better at this. False signals and easily misinterpreted patterns could lead an investor into penury.

For instance, one task is to assess whether the current trend is likely to continue – if you are in a boom market, will the euphoria continue long enough for you to buy the shares and reap the benefits? In a soggy bear market the trick is to predict when it is likely to turn up again. This is made all the harder by the short fluctuations within the longer-term movements. Or as the distinguished economist Sir Alec Cairncross put it:

> A trend (to use the language of Gertrude Stein) is a trend is a trend.
> But the question is: will it bend?
> Will it alter its course,
> Through some unforeseen force,
> And come to a premature end?

The second problem is that if they were really helpful, they would get widely adopted, other investors would rely on the developing pattern and the self-fulfilling prophecies would run away before the amateur could get involved. There would also be repeated attempts to spot the direction of development before it was complete, which would distort the shapes and cause confusion.

Professionals do not rely on charts as the trigger or guidance, but use them as an adjunct to other investment criteria. What this all boils down to is trying to get additional help on timing. That means timing not just for the individual company but also for the sector and the market as a whole. This applies with equal force on when to sell (see Chapter 26). A measure of how well priced the shares are is the yield gap: the difference between the yield on ordinary shares and the return to maturity of gilts (see Chapter 3).

CHARTS

Charts are a useful adjunct for the private investor because for once there is parity with the professionals. Both have access to the same information and it is just the skill at interpreting the data that makes the difference. But just as there are swarms of people with their own pet theories on how to pick the winners, so there are fanatical chartists looking for the philosopher's stone. Their greatest value is to focus the mind on the fact that in a market the correct price is what somebody is prepared to pay, so charts do provide a bit of discipline for private investors by making them concentrate on supply and demand, price and timing.

Lines

For successful predictions you have to be able to recognize the patterns that any of these lines follow. There are the overall trends, for instance – up, down or sideways – detectable by joining the peaks and troughs (or bar tips) of the fluctuating lines of prices. In a sideways market, when the price oscillates between two horizontal lines, a wise chartist waits for a 'breakout' signal when the price finally shows which way the market is now going to go.

One answer is not to worry if the share is taking a favourable long-term path. For instance, take a company with shares notoriously volatile – it may look like a sideways movement but the two trend lines are a long way apart. The price bounces up and down on rumour and gloom, or profit-taking and bargain-hunting, without any obvious long-term direction. For an alert investor that can provide a nice little earner. Just examine when and by how much it tends to oscillate and just keep hopping in at the bottom and out at the top. This is safer in largish companies, which also means the gains will not be enormous, so the deals have to be large enough to offset dealing costs.

The chart patterns have graphic names to help. A 'support area' can be detected by the price dropping to but constantly rebounding from a specific price level, and there is an upward equivalent called a 'resistance level'. If the market breaks up through the established resistance level, chartists reckon the price will rise substantially to a new high, and similarly in reverse for breaking through a support level.

There are also 'double tops', which as you would expect have twin peaks and indicate an imminent drop, with a 'double bottom' being the upside-down equivalent, A 'head and shoulders' is a peak flanked by two smaller peaks and indicates the reversal of an upward trend, signalling an imminent fall. Understandably a 'reversed head and shoulders' is the same thing upside down, forecasting a rise.

Flags are parallelograms with a mast down at least one side when a sharp change is followed by a sideways fluctuation within a narrow range. If the flag is preceded by a rise it is usually by another rise and a fall is followed by a further fall.

Triangles are pretty self-explanatory. The share price oscillates through a steadily smaller range. When it finally breaks out of the pattern, the direction is said to be an indicator of the way it will move for a time.

If a share has been wobbling along for a long time between two constant limits, it is said to be in a channel and, once again, breaking out of it is normally an indication of the new direction that the price is now likely to take.

A wealth of other patterns can be detected by the practised and imaginative chartist and they all give some signal about the future direction of prices.

Point and figure

One variant is the 'point and figure' chart (see page 134). This concentrates on just price movements to focus the mind when there is a shift from buying to selling or vice versa.

Point and figure charts select an appropriate amount of price change that is worth recording, say 5p. If the share rises by that amount the chart shows an x; another rise of that amount and another x is stacked above the first and so on until the price changes direction. Then the chartist moves to the next column and, one square down from the line of crosses, puts an o. If it drops another 5p there will be another o beneath that and so on. A reversal starts a new line one square up with an x. The chart ignores time, though chartists usually put the number of the month of a new stack at the top and bottom – 1 for January, 2 for February, etc – and usually start a new year with a new stack.

Candlesticks

Another type of chart, which used to be called 'bar charts' has now been dubbed 'candlesticks' as the technique has gained interest in recent years (see page 135). It is actually much older than Dow's theories, having been used by Japanese rice traders for centuries, but works on the same assumptions: price changes move in patterns that recur and hence are predictable. Despite a small but devoted following among some professionals, including currency traders, this is widely ignored by people discussing investment. You will not for instance find an entry for it in many even relatively recent dictionaries of investing or finance.

The chart shows the opening and closing prices for each day, as well as the highest and lowest prices reached during the day. Just as the occidental charts have names for regular or significant patterns, so does this, but in characteristic oriental fashion they are rather picturesque, fey sorts of labels. There are things called

```
                          GLAXOSMITHKLINE
BOX REVERSAL 3 BOX SIZE £ 20              DAILY DATA      22/ 6/98 TO 22/ 6/01

    2300....................................................................................
                          X
                          XO
                          XO
                          XO
    2200................XOX.....X........................................................
                          XOXO      XO
                          XOXO      XO
                          XO OX     XO
                          X  OXO    XO
    2100................X..OXO..XO.............................................X
                          1  OXO    40                                        X
                          X  OXO    XO                                   O    X X
                          X  OXO    XO                                   XOX XOX
                          X  2XO    XO                          X      X  X XOXOXON
    2000................X..OXOX.XO.............................XO..X...XO..XOXOXOXO.
                       X X  OX3XOXO                             XOX XO  XOX XOXO OX
               X       X XOX OXOXOXOX                           XOX5XO  XO8OXOX  OX
               XO      XDXOX OXOXOXOXO                         X X XOXOXO 7OXOX9X  O
               XO      XOXO  OXOXOXOXO              X          XOXOXO OXOX XOXOXOX
    1900.....XO......XOX...0.0.OXOXO....X.............XD.........XOXOX..OXOXOXOXO.0.......
           X X XOX      XO         0 OXO    XO         X XO      XOXOX OX6XOXOX
           70X8XOXO     N          0 0      XO         XOXO    X XOXOX  0 OXO OX
           XOXOXOXOX X X            OX  XOX            XOXO    XOXO OX   OX  OX
           XOXOXO OXOXOX  1         5XO  XOXO          NO 0    XOX  0    OX  OX
    1800.60XOX..OXOXOX...9.........OXOX.XOXO........X.X..0..X....X04........OX..0..........
         XOXOX 9XOXOX    9        OXOXOXOXO         XOX  0  XO    XOX       OX
         OXOX  0 0 OX    9        0 OXOXOXO         XOX  0  XO    XOX       0
         OXO       OX            0 06070X           XO    OX XO   XOX
         OX        OX            0 0 OXO    X X     OX1XO  XO
    1700..0.........OX......................OXO..X.XOX....OXOX0....X....................
                   OX                      OXO  XOXOX  OXO 0   X
                   OX                      OXO  X09OX  OX  0   X
                   OX                      OXO  XO OX  0   0   X
                   OX                      0 OX X  OX      OX  X
    1600...........OX.....................OXOX..OX.......OX2X.X...................
                   OX                      080X  OX       OXOXOX
                   OX                      0 OX  0        OXOXOX
                   OX                       OX           2 0 OXOX
                   0                        0           0   030
    1500.........................................0....OX.......................
                                           0   OX
                                           OX
                                           OX
                                           0
    1400..................................................................................
```

Figure 18.1 A point and figure chart

three black crows and three advancing soldiers, shootings stars, morning and evening stars, hanging man, hammers, and so on. These charts show how trading went. So, for instance, if there is a lot of wick above the candle there must have been a rally during the day that failed to hold and will have discouraged traders. Conversely a length of wick dangling out of the bottom (called the hammer) shows an abundance of sellers threatened to push the market down but there were more than enough buyers to offset that so the market bounced off the bottom, which gives promise of further rises. The wick of each candle runs from the

Figure 18.2 A candlestick chart

low to the high reached. The wider body of the candle is between the opening and closing prices – if the closing price is lower than the opening the candle is black, if higher it is white (the original Japanese version used red for these).

SENTIMENT INDICATORS

Technical analysis is not just about charts. There are hosts of other indicators providing additional or alternative pointers to market movements and hence tips on when to trade.

At one time one popular guide – at least in the United States – was the 'small-lot indicator'. This works on the assumption that small investors are almost invariably wrong. They buy at the top and sell at the bottom, so they provide a good counter-indicator. This has been gradually extended as it became clear it was not just the amateurs who got carried away by the prevailing or fashionable economic view. So it became slightly transformed to the feeling that a universally bearish attitude in the country as a whole is a sign of an upturn and rampant bullishness is a sign to sell. Some companies even tabulate the number of investment advisers that are bullish or bearish as a sign to go the other way when unanimity seems imminent. The flow of funds indicators shows demand for securities and where people are heading to put their cash.

One of the difficulties with any of these guides of course is that as soon as they become generally known they fail to provide reliable signals. The combination of price and volume movements gives a pretty good indication of overall attitudes:

- if prices and the amounts of shares traded are both rising, it is an indication that the market for the share is set to rise;
- a rising price but declining volume of shares traded is a worrying trend, indicating that the price rise is running out of steam and as the upward movement slows to a halt, the direction is likely to reverse and the price will soon start to fall;
- a falling price coupled with rising volume shows investors heading for the exit in growing numbers, which can only reinforce and accelerate the falling price;
- the price and volume of shares traded both falling shows investors beginning to have second thoughts about selling and the downward pressure is therefore easing; soon it will bottom out and start upwards.

OTHER THEORIES

There are many other systems attempting to predict market movements. Like any other activity in areas dominated by luck and the unpredictable, such as fishing and acting for instance, there is quite lot of superstition involved. People are ready to grasp at any apparent correlation, no matter how dubious.

So there is one theory that sunny weather produces an optimism in people generally that is reflected in prices, and another view has it that the market index moves up and down with skirt hemlines. Another old adage was, 'Sell in May and go away' on the assumption that everybody went away for the summer and in the absence of trade, activity was listless and random. In fact any investigation shows the saying to have been unjustified when coined and becoming less reliable since.

Finally, do not buy on a tip or rumour. It is most unlikely that you will be the first to hear it, even if it is true, and there is a very good chance it is unjustified gossip or a 'ramp' – somebody starting a story to shove up the price of shares he or she wants to sell. On the other hand, if it really is true and the information comes from someone on the inside, acting on it could land you in jail for insider trading.

19 | What is a stock market?

The stock market is not in its fundamentals greatly different from the New Covent Garden, Smithfield or Billingsgate. Whether you are dealing in turnips, pork or haddock, or the shares of Marks & Spencer, it is just a matter of buyers, sellers, an agreed price, and usually a middleman. And just as the food markets do not encourage people to amble in and ask for half a pound of carrots, so the stock exchange is nervous about private investors poking into its electronics and therefore requires an intermediary to feed the investors' instructions into the computer.

In Britain the first recorded joint-stock company was founded in 1553 to finance an expedition to the Orient via a northeast passage. Two of the ships sheltered from storms in northern Scandinavia and all the officers and crew froze to death. The third managed to reach Archangel and then went overland to Moscow – which was as near to the Orient as they got – where the Czar Ivan the Terrible agreed a trading link. That seemed good enough: it created business confidence, so others followed the technique for raising money. There have been some unfortunate incidents since. Probably the best known is the South Sea Bubble. This came from the mad enthusiasm over a company that took over the national debt in return for having a monopoly of trade in the Pacific. The shares reached a price of £1,050 each before a realization that good living and share ramping seemed a higher priority for the board than trade. That caused the bubble and the company to burst and led to a long series of dominos toppling behind it as banks, shops and individuals went bust as a result. In fact it was only one of many insubstantial companies whose shares soared out of sight.

Like so many of London's financial establishments, the London Stock Exchange grew out of a coffee house – others include Lloyd's and the Baltic Exchange – in this case the New Jonathan's coffee rooms. As business grew they first moved out of the coffee house and then into a succession of larger premises and in 1801 acquired the name of Stock Exchange. There used to be 20 other exchanges around the country but they were amalgamated into the one at Old Broad Street next to the Bank of England. The rather grand building is now almost wholly superfluous – it does not even house the computer that looks after the trading.

The London Stock Exchange has two main components, the first being the official list, which is the main market of major companies. This is divided up into groupings by trade. So there is a section for distribution, one for banks, another for breweries, plus one called Techmark (or techMARK as the stock exchange calls it in an attempt at trendiness at least in its typography) for high-tech companies. In addition, there is the Alternative Investment Market (see Chapter 20), which is for young companies that do not have the trading record demanded for a full listing.

One important difference from the world of meat and veg is that in stock markets one is at several stages removed from the real world. It is not just that the shares represent an interest in a company that may be miles away or even overseas, but increasingly there is not even a scrap of paper to show the ownership of that interest, merely a computer record somewhere. And as the trading becomes increasingly electronic, with trading from one's desktop computer and the payment being just another electronic instruction to transfer funds, it is becoming more of a computer game.

Where stock markets used to have physical presence where people met and haggled about deals, electronics has liberated them; now the market is everywhere and nowhere. This is presenting the authorities with an increasingly difficult task in monitoring, and presents the investor with a growing challenge to make sure the deal is authentic, the price is right and the securities really are being transferred. The way all this works is in a state of transition, with the mergers of European exchanges.

London's main market operates on a computerized system called the Stock Exchange Electronic Trading System (SETS) for large shares, with a modified version for mid-market companies. SETS is an order-matching system that tries to pair off the instructions posted to the machine by buyers and sellers.

For the moment the smaller shares are still using a system called SEAQ, which is based on a program evolved for an American exchange.

The completed deal is passed to yet another computer to organize settlement. The Crest system is trying to eliminate the blizzard of paper by replacing share certificates with an electronic record in much the same way that one's hoard of gold and cash has been transformed into an item in a bank's computer memory. For the mistrustful and Luddite investors, share certificates are still available.

Many of the execution-only brokers try to simplify life by putting their investors' holdings into a 'nominee account'. That means the shares are registered to one broker's account in the stock exchange's and the companies' share registers, which makes the deals quicker and cheaper. The only drawback is the ultimate holder having problems voting at annual general meetings or getting shareholder perks.

There are other markets – see Chapters 20 and 21. There is Ofex, which has its own list of shares, and there is Virt-X, which provides an electronic market in shares (and is itself listed on Aim). Several Internet-based exchanges are getting off the ground, though acceptance is taking some time. On top of all that there are the overseas exchanges, from Amsterdam and Frankfurt to New York and Tokyo.

20 | Other UK markets

THE ALTERNATIVE INVESTMENT MARKET

Usually known by its initials, this is actually merely a division of
the stock market reserved for smaller businesses. The idea is that
eventually they mature, grow and graduate onto the main market. So it is sometimes rather pretentiously called the 'cadet
branch' of the stock market. That means younger companies with
a less solid or shorter record of profits are allowed to join. Given
that the costs for the business of getting on to Aim are almost as
high as for the full listing, the main attraction is the lower hurdle
and access to the market publicity. The market has proved more
popular than sceptics expected and about 750 companies from
many countries have joined, raising £8.5 billion, and it has been
attracting 40 per cent of the flotations by Western Europe's smaller
companies.

For the smaller investor in Britain the attraction has been
increased by Aim-listed companies being regarded by the Inland
Revenue as unquoted. This provides access to different types of
tax relief, including business taper and gift relief for capital gains
tax, suitability for the Enterprise Investment Scheme, relief for
losses and business property relief for inheritance tax.

On the other hand, one drawback is that smaller companies are
more vulnerable to financial problems. They also go in and out of
fashion with the institutional investors who set the market tone.
The latter can however provide an opportunity for the shrewd
opportunist who can recognize a temporary movement by the
herd of institutional sheep and nip in for a bit of counter-fashion-
able profit, whether buying shares in companies currently feared
by the big boys, or selling when the enthusiasm has been exces-
sive.

That provides an opportunity for the small investor. Shrewd opportunists who spotted the Internet stocks as having a good future when they first appeared on the Aim market made a massive amount of money: some shares rose tenfold in a matter of days. It is no guarantee though, because smaller companies are generally more vulnerable to problems.

TECHMARK

Worried at the criticism that the stock market was irrelevant to new companies and that it gave no help to high-technology businesses that are about to provide the future wealth of the country, the London Stock Exchange launched a section or index in its market called Techmark (or techMARK as its own typography has it).

The principal aim of this sector is to attract companies involved with new technical ideas – including the Internet – with the promise of rapid growth. As the literature points out, buying shares in this area is considerably more risky since many of the so-called businesses are little more than a bright idea, and many of them have never seen profits.

OFEX

This is one of the growing number of competitors to the main London stock market. A contraction of 'off-exchange', the Ofex system was started in 1995 and trade is done on a computer owned by stockbroker J Jenkins. It is a matched-bargain system, so the deal only goes through if there is another willing buyer/seller feeding an order into the machine with a similar view on prices. Being a matched-bargain system the fees can be pretty low. It has some substantial companies traded on it including National Parking and Weetabix.

VIRT-X

This incorporates a midget rival to the London stock exchange called Tradepoint, which started as an electronic order book in 1995 and was itself quoted on Aim. In combination with the Swiss exchange, SWX, it created Virt-X, with offices in London and Zurich and backing from American investment banks.

In addition to trading in the normal UK quoted stocks (though it has only about 1 per cent of the total trade), it has set up clearance and registry systems to allow trading in Eurotop, the 300 largest companies in Europe.

21 | Other markets

NASDAQ

Nasdaq is the acronym for the National Association of Securities Dealers Automated Quotation system. It is second only to the New York Stock Exchange (often called the Big Board) as the largest stock market in the United States and is one of the four big ones in the world, together with Tokyo and London. As it has kept costs of entry and administrative demands comparatively low, many young companies, especially in technology, have opted to be quoted there, including Internet companies like Amazon. Some, like Microsoft, Dell and Intel, stayed there despite their subsequent growth.

It has fought back against the threat of the Internet-based share trading systems by forging alliances with some of them. There is a growing number of such schemes, including ones run by Bloomberg, Reuters and MarketXT. The computer-based systems can post quotes and execute trades on Nasdaq Intermarket, including in shares quoted on the New York stock exchange.

INTERNET

In addition to the opportunities for cheap and convenient access to stockbrokers via a home computer, there is no real reason why the stock market itself should not be a part of the World Wide Web. However, investors bypassing the exchanges and dealing directly with each other is distinctly dodgier. The main obstacle is uncertainty: it is hard to know who really is at the other end of the deal and whether the money or shares really are available, and if they are not how one could enforce the contract legally or recover the money. None of this is insuperable and no doubt mechanisms can be developed from online credit checks, through interrogating share registers to certificated electronic signatures, but it may be a few years yet before it is all working efficiently.

In the meantime electronic trading exchanges may emerge first. The Internet is continuously providing new opportunities. Two market facilities already running are called Posit and Instinet; they are principally for institutional investors, but others are promised or at trial stages.

There is also talk of disintermediation (cutting out the middleman) by companies raising capital. Raising money by a public issue of shares is a costly business for a company, not least in the enormous fees to accountants, lawyers, stockbrokers and merchant banks. It would be attractive if all this could be bypassed by making the shares available over the Net. Small investors for their part seldom get their hands on new issues because they are snapped up before they get there, or more often companies opt for the cheaper route of placing the issue with institutions. It can be dodgy for the investor, however, since there will be less assurance that the professionals have crawled over the business to check its figures, managers and promises, and it is difficult to tell from the puff appearing on the screen whether a company even exists as described, much less whether its managers are competent and honest.

People are understandably reluctant to get involved in an area rife with unseen dangers. But it is changing rapidly. Customers happy to see a waiter disappear with their credit card for 20 minutes without worrying whether he is nipping up the road for a shopping spree are also prepared to read their card number out to some unknown person at the other of the telephone for an order. These people are now increasingly buying books, CDs, holiday tickets and the like on the Net and relatively few have been ripped off.

From time to time there are tales of pimply schoolboys extracting credit card numbers from online traders, but few people have lost money as a consequence and it is a lot rarer than having your car stolen or your house burgled. The danger of some hacker getting into you computer or dealing at your expense is pretty remote. Viruses are a hazard but can be avoided by having a continuously updated virus checker, which applies to anyone who goes onto the Net.

There are about 1½ million online stockbroking accounts in Europe and the number is growing fast. Many of these people have little loyalty to any broker or market, but will trade where it is safe, cheap and convenient.

EMERGING MARKETS

Then there are the 'emerging markets'. The term is generally used for the small, fledgling stock exchanges in Eastern Europe like Poland, Russia, Hungary, the Czech Republic, in the Far East like Indonesia and Korea, in South America, and in places like Turkey. Sometimes these markets perform spectacularly well and sometimes plunge equally spectacularly.

22 | Do share- holders have any rights or duties?

SPECIFIC RIGHTS

Shareholders are the true owners of the company, and they have lots of rights as a result. For a start, they in theory appoint both the board of directors and the auditors. In practice the directors do both, and shareholders have all too often supinely agreed to everything done in their name. Even great institutional holders who know the law and accounting principles and are sophisticated investors, have been lax in exerting their power and have generally more often sold the shares than spoken up or done anything for the business. This has been changing: some are using their influence and it is becoming less easy for a chairman to dismiss awkward questions at the annual meeting, but still too many private individuals consider any questioning of the board as an unseemly delay of their free drinks.

As owners, shareholders are also entitled to be given a wide range of information, and to participate in the company's success.

Information

The information the owners must have includes regular financial facts. Every year the company must produce an account of its finances (the phrasing in law is a little more complicated but that is what the rules amount to) and this must be sent to all registered shareholders. (See Chapter 14 for what the useful information is in those annual reports and accounts and how to extract it.) Shareholders must also have notice of important events affecting the business; this includes details of major acquisitions and disposals, demergers and reorganizations.

Annual general meeting

The annual general meeting is a legal obligation and shareholders must be notified in advance of its time and place. There is however no legal insistence that the meeting is held in a convenient spot, so if the directors are feeling bloody-minded they could hold it in the upstairs room of a pub on Stornoway. Curious times and inconvenient places for meetings, plus company announcements on Christmas Eve are good signs to shareholders that all is not well with the business.

At the AGM shareholders are called on to approve the accounts by voting, can ask questions, and have a vote on a number of other resolutions including the reappointment of auditors and directors. Most shareholders neglect this privilege, either throwing away the voting card altogether or just sending back the enclosed proxy form giving the chairman carte blanche to vote on their behalf.

Consultation

There is a legal obligation to consult shareholders on matters that affect the company's future. They have the right to vote on major decisions, including actions that may dilute their holdings such as rights issues and employee share option schemes. They are asked annually to approve the reappointment of the auditors (see Chapter 14). They have to approve the appointment of directors, and when there is a normal re-election process they have to confirm them in their jobs.

If shareholders can muster 5 per cent of the company's equity or 100 of them get together, they can even introduce their own resolutions at the meeting.

Dividends

Shareholders are entitled to take part in the company's success and profits. Normally shareholders participate in the company's profits by way of dividends, which are usually paid twice a year. But this is not a legal right since a company may decide to reinvest its profits in the business for faster growth. In practice few have the courage to refrain from paying. The cheque or notification of payment into an account shows the size of holding and rate of dividend. Preference shares are normally entitled to a dividend, and if the company cannot for a time afford to pay, that entitlement is only deferred and has to be paid later when the money is available.

Scrip issues

Sometimes a company prefers to pay some or all of its dividend in new shares instead of cash. That can create problems for shareholders in the calculation of the cost of a stake and so the capital gains tax to be paid on disposal (see also Chapter 27).

Rights issues

Some schemes to raise more money for company expansion involve giving the existing shareholders the right of first refusal. For details see the next chapter.

Extraordinary general meeting

Shareholders may demand the convening of an extraordinary general meeting.

Nominee accounts

Many people hold their shares in nominee accounts – for PEPs and ISAs they have to. These are held in a number of places and are a convenience to prevent shuffling of papers or to speed the processes of buying and selling. For instance, the dealing stockbroker may hold an account for an investor who does not therefore have to wait for share certificates to arrive before being able to sell them, and does not have to store and find scraps of necessary paper. Some brokers offer the service free as a way of reducing their own administration; some charge a flat fee or one based on the value of the shares, others charge per transaction, and some large companies have instituted their own systems.

The nominee is the legal owner of the shares, although they are held beneficially for the investor. There are inconveniences of holding shares this way. For example, the real owners lose the right to vote or ask questions at general meetings. In addition, they will not get the annual report, though the administrator of the nominee holding will normally forward it if asked, and in some cases they have lost the windfall bonuses when mutual organizations like building societies become quoted companies. They are also likely to be excluded from shareholder perks. Many companies have relented and will allow beneficial holders to get the perks once the nominee has written to the registrar to identify the beneficiary.

REGULATED MARKETS

In addition to their rights in relation to the company of which they own a piece, investors have a right not be ripped off by the financial community. This is the part that is mainly watched over by the Financial Services Authority. It regulates British brokers and dealers, whether they are in a City office or dealing via the Internet, but nobody regulates the Internet. Inevitably the Net has been a happy playground for shady operators, ranging from various types of fraudsters to people operating pyramid schemes. Some have set up bogus Web sites to look like the pages operated by real investment companies, in the hope of getting unsuspecting people to part with money. In addition, the Net is awash with rumours, many of them carefully placed to drive the price up or down so the instigator can sell or buy and make a killing. The authorities in the more responsible countries pursue these people, but the Net is too vast to be watched.

The Financial Services Authority also supervises the established stock markets: the main London Stock Exchange, Ofex and Virt-X. It also looks after the listings and requirements for the main market companies and has responsibility for investigating abuses of the market. That means it watches the sophisticated computer program which tries to spot unusual trading patterns and if there are suspicious movements prior to an official announcement (such as just before a bid or the announcement of unexpected trading results), it investigates. Prosecutions however have been rare and convictions even rarer. The Stock Exchange itself still regulates the admission and disclosure requirements for companies on the Alternative Investment Market.

Relying on somebody else to pick up the pieces and fight the battles for feckless or foolish investors is wrong. A little elementary care can prevent a lot of mistakes and save a lot of effort trying to assert one's rights later. For instance, you should use only authorized businesses to act on your behalf, and that is easy to check on the register of the Financial Services Authority. Before starting any transactions, check the costs and fees. The first rule is, if there is anything you do not understand go on asking for an explanation until it is crystal clear. It is a lot better to seem foolish by asking questions than to be foolish by not having the answers.

CODES OF CONDUCT

The apathy of most shareholders has allowed company boards so much latitude that they seemed beyond reasonable control. To fill this vacuum the City has produced a series of codes of conduct to guide directors on best practice. There were the reports from the Cadbury, Greenburg, Hampel and Higgs committees, all of which advocated a strengthening of the corporate governance requirements. They suggested that:

▌ the task of chairman and chief executive should be separate;
▌ directors should stand for re-election every three years;
▌ board members should not have a service contract of more

than two years;

- a third of the board should be non-executives who should be independent of the company;
- shareholders should be told at least 20 days in advance of an annual general meeting;
- when raising new capital the company should give existing investors first refusal;
- any questions not answered at the annual general meeting should receive written answers soon afterwards;
- executive directors should have no more than one non-executive directorship and should not be chairman of another major company – and no individual should chair more than one major company;
- a chief executive should not become chairman of the same company;
- the performance of the board, its committees and its individual members, should be evaluated at least once a year;
- non-executive directors should normally serve two three-year terms;
- non-executive directors should not hold share options in their company;
- a resigning non-executive director should tell the board why.

23 | What are rights and scrip issues?

RIGHTS

Companies wanting to raise additional capital sometimes turn to existing shareholders first. There are several reasons for this. The first is obvious: shareholders by definition must like the company, so if it says it can see opportunities for useful investment to allow it to grow but needs additional cash, they are more likely to take a friendly view. Second, it is only fair to allow existing holders to take action against having their holdings diluted by the issue of further shares. Third, the institutions that own about four-fifths of the shares on issue in Britain are especially insistent about being given the chance to maintain the percentage of the company they had decided was right for that portfolio – this is called their pre-emption right.

It is a long and expensive business for a company, since it must print extensive literature and post it to all shareholders, and the merchant banks and accountants cost a fortune in fees. A placing – ringing round funds known to be interested and asking if they would like to buy extra shares – works out a lot cheaper and can be very quick.

The opportunity to buy the new shares is allocated as a ratio of existing shares owned. It is something like the right to buy three new shares for every 11 already held or some such formula, depending on how much the company is trying to raise and how deep a discount it is offering. The issue will dilute the value of the existing shares because profits and dividends will be distributed over a larger number of shares.

Rights issues are normally issued at a discount to the prevailing share price to give people the illusion that they are getting a bargain. If the shares stand at 200p, the company might offer one new share for every four already held at a price of 150p. So for every four shares, worth £8, they can buy another for £1.50. If they do buy they have a holding worth £9.50 (assuming the price does not move). But the market price, adjusted for the dilution and the price paid would be less than that (excluding the other vagaries of the stock market and its reaction to the share issue). The four continuing shares would be worth £7.60 (four-fifths of £9.50), but on that calculation the right would be worth 40p, so they would be back to the original £8 holding. One complication is that the money received for the rights may be taxable, and another is that the market price will react to the announcement.

Shareholders faced with a rights issue can take it up in full and pay for the new issue of shares. They can sell the nil-paid rights that have a value on the stock market. Or they can compromise by selling enough nil-paid rights to maintain the value of the portfolio by using the proceeds to buy new shares. The nil-paid price is the difference between the discounted rights issue share price and the ex-rights price.

SCRIP ISSUES

This looks like a burst of spontaneous generosity by companies giving investors some extra shares for nothing. Sometimes they are in place of cash dividends and sometimes as a supplement to them.

In fact it is a simple bookkeeping exercise that should have no effect on the share price or the value of the company – some of the retained earnings are capitalized and shifted from one line in the books to another. That is also the reason they are called 'capitalization issues'. Sometimes they are also called a 'bonus issue' and surprisingly enough, contrary to logic, the share price sometimes rises at the same time.

24 | What do you do at takeovers?

Usually, you say thank you very much. Bids for companies are almost invariably well above the price of the shares just before, so shareholders tend to benefit. On the other hand, what may well have tempted a predator is precisely that the price was standing way below any rational basis of valuation, for instance the net asset value, so it would be worth buying a business just to sell off its assets at a profit. In that case it is worth resisting, if only to get a better price.

Sometimes the target company resists the offer fiercely, and the scheme for some inverted reason is then called a hostile takeover. The defence usually says the bid is unwelcome and opportunistic and the company could perform far better on its own given the chance. The private shareholder cannot tell whether this opposition is motivated by a desire for independence, a fear of directors losing their jobs, an attempt to get the bidder to increase the price, or a genuine feeling shareholders would do better with the existing regime.

The decision is made even more complicated if the offer is wholly or in part in the form of the bidder's shares. The choice is then cluttered with other considerations such as whether one wants those shares, whether the valuation of the buyer's equity is fair or realistic, and whether selling might crystallize an unwelcome capital gains tax liability.

The takeover process is monitored by the City Takeover Panel, which has no power, legal or otherwise, but manages to have its way because all the City people support it. So anybody who tries to flout its rulings would be ostracized, and once frozen out of the financial community doing business would be impossible. Being non-statutory also gives the panel the signal advantage of being able to act quickly. Moreover it can tell participants it does not like the way they are acting – it has been known to reprimand people not for failing to follow the letter of the City code but for neglecting its spirit. In addition it can take instant action to change the code when a loophole has been discovered.

It can be almost as good to own shares in a company that is in the same sector as a highly publicized acquisition. As soon as one estate agent, retailer, computer assembler, brewer or whatever has been bought, the market assumes a ripple of parallel acquisition activity will overtake its competitors. Their shares jump as a result. Since the flurry of copycat activity only sometimes materializes, especially once the targets have become expensive, it may then be a good time to sell.

25 | What if the company goes bust?

Investing in shares is risky. There is no way of getting away from this. One of the reasons the stock market produces a higher average return than, say, putting the money into a building society is to offset this danger by compensating investors. But note the word 'average'. Some shares are more risky than others and short of buying into hundreds of companies, the investor will be involved in shares that are a mixture: successful – if lucky some of them spectacularly so – pretty ho-hum, and some complete collapses, which are spectacular, but rare.

Occasionally collapses are signalled well ahead. The shares show a steep and pretty well continuous slide and the statements from the company mix profits warnings with promises of restructuring, refinancing, a search for alliances, the appointment of new executives and the promise of new policies on the way. This usually ends in a suspension of dealings in the shares. That move is usually said to be to help shareholders. Pure bunkum: it is a complete disaster for shareholders who cannot therefore sell shares at any price to rescue even a tiny portion of their investment money. The people it helps are the stock market traders who are fearful of dealing without adequate information and cannot face being swamped by people stampeding out of the company.

Companies seldom return from that sort of suspension. There are other reasons for suspension, such as during the final stages of a major acquisition, but those really are benign and are to prevent total market chaos when there is not enough known about the deal details to set a fair price. But from suspension due to the company having run out of money, there are few roads back.

By the time the shares are suspended they are seldom worth more than a few pence in any case. But not all collapses are so well signposted. Are there any more covert signs of impending doom that canny shareholders may be able to spot? Many people have tried drawing up signs, including Britain's top liquidator in the 1960s, Bill Mackie. The specifics of his warning signals indicating flamboyant headquarters and profligate top management may now seem dated, but the underlying principles are still sound. We may no longer have flagpoles and tanks of tropical fish but there are plenty of other loud signals that the organization thinks appearance more important than efficiency.

Investors should be monitoring the business and how it is managed; see Chapters 14 and 15 for the various calculations indicating the state of corporate health. Profit margins are a good sign, so one should check whether they are as high as they were and at least as great as those at other similar companies, and whether the business is generating sufficient cash for its needs and ambitions. When external money is being raised through loans, rights issues and the like, they should be for expansion rather than baling out the current problems. Accountants reporting late, auditors' qualifications, suggestions of window-dressing in the accounts and extremely sophisticated financial dealings are causes of concern. With small businesses most of that does not apply and you have little recourse but to judge by the managers. The point about small businesses is that the profit can be spectacular but the collapses sudden.

When a company's share dealings have been suspended, it is commonly a sign that the company's managers, bankers and set of insolvency accountants have gone into a confab. One route is for the company to try for a voluntary arrangement under which its creditors hold off knocking bits off the corporate structure to sell as a way of recovering their money, and allow it to try trading its way out of its problems. Courts can appoint an administrator who also continues to trade and holds off creditors.

Secured creditors, normally the banks, who have run out of patience with the company's excuses and are worried their loans could soon become irrecoverable, take another route. They appoint a receiver with the sole task of keeping the business going just long enough to recover the banks' money. Tax authorities have also been pretty active in this route to make sure their money is paid. Occasionally the directors ask for the appointment because they can see a default on debts looming up or because they are in danger of 'overtrading', which is the criminal offence of continuing in business once the company is insolvent. A specialist accountant is then appointed and moves in to run the business briefly to extract some money or sell assets for paying the debt. In theory he then moves out and the company reverts to business as usual. This seldom happens in practice because the receiver's task entails selling off the assets against which the money was lent, or trading long enough for the cash to pay off the loan. That usually does not leave much and the company is often passed to a liquidator.

As that name implies, the liquidator's job is to turn anything saleable into something more liquid like cash. Fire sales like this seldom produce anything like the book value of the assets.

In all of these procedures there is a hierarchy of creditor, and the holder of ordinary shares ranks at the end of the line. The government has taken its taxes off the top, but is about to join the other creditors in the queue, and is followed by secured lenders with a claim on the property, and the banks with other guarantees. Then there are bondholders and owners of preference shares. Once all these people have had their pickings there is seldom anything left for the holders of ordinary shares.

The one comforting thought is that relatively few quoted companies do actually go bust. And if your investment happens nevertheless to be one of them, try and look for the silver lining: you can cash in some really profitable investment to set off the capital gains against the losses on the crashed company.

26 | When do you sell a share?

V S Naipaul, in his book *A Bend in the River,* wrote:

> A businessman is someone who buys at ten and is happy get out at twelve. The other kind of man buys at ten, sees it rise to eighteen and does nothing. He is waiting for it to rise to twenty. When it drops to two he waits for it to get back to ten.

He has clearly observed naive investors well. For some time New York professional investors used the 'small lot indicator' (trades in small values of shares) as a useful counter-indicator. In other words, when the small buyers started piling in it was time to sell and vice versa. The news got around, and so many people started acting on the theory that it became a self-defeating prophecy and became a positive guide until confusion seems to have buried it.

Deciding when to sell is just as crucial as picking the time to buy, and just as tricky.

SOME THEORIES

Just as there are innumerable theories about how to select a share, so there are endless formulae for when to buy and sell (see also Chapter 18). One theory holds that share selection is for the long term, so there is little point in reacting to every whim of stock market fashion. You bought for the long term, so hold on. This is an apparently sensible approach that can provide a useful overall guide, but it ignores the realities of life. For instance, the assumption that dictated the original decision may no longer apply – the company, the economy or the portfolio may have changed. So it is worth reviewing the decision from time to time.

Some of the guides to investment say fatuous things like, 'sell your worst shares early'. But if it were that easy to tell which the worst shares are, one would not be reading a book – just because a share has dropped and another risen does not mean they will continue in the same direction, as lots of price charts clearly show. Some old market hands are always against buying a plunging share in the hope of recovery – 'the market is trying to tell you something', they say. But if, for instance, a share goes from 23p to £12.40 in the space of 18 months and then drops back to 60p in the next six months, when did the market get it right?

So there are no obvious answers. Anybody claiming to have a simple explanation is a fool or a liar. If it were that easy everybody would have done it long ago.

There are mathematical theories about what you should do. They are interesting, some have been programmed into computers, but none of them can be justified on any logical basis. One suggests selling shares after they have fallen 8 per cent; another says sell when they have dropped 7 per cent below the top price reached.

CASHING PROFITS

'It is never wrong to take a profit' is one of the ancient rules of stock market investment. Yes, the share price may go on zooming up still further, but your profit is safe. One alternative when winning is to hedge your bets by selling part of the holding to recover the original investment plus a bit of profit, and let the rest ride just in case there is further growth left. Another of the hallowed sayings of the market comes to much the same thing: 'leave some profit for the other chap'. This is deeply reassuring stuff and eases the irritation of selling when the share continues to rise, but just consider the odds against being able to buy at the bottom and sell at the top.

REDUCING LOSSES

By some curious chance, most of the advice from professionals is about how to secure your profit. The assumption is that nobody ever buys a dud. There is less helpful advice about when to join the other sleek rats heading for the shore.

In falling markets private shareholders fall into two opposing camps. There is the one Naipaul described, who hangs on to the most obvious rubbish in the hope it will eventually recover. Then there is the sort who panic at any serious drop and bail out in the expectation that once heading downwards, the law of gravity will continue to operate. Both are probably wrong.

The point about private investment is that it is generally for the longish term. So the buyer should have done some pretty careful research on the business before buying its shares. The corollary is that if it continues to meet those criteria (eg, good management, reasonable margins, innovation, good financial control, etc), then it may well be a good idea to hang on and just go on collecting dividends. On the other hand, that also means the investor must continue with the work, to see if the company is still up to snuff and therefore worth backing. If not, sell.

So much for cashing in profits or preventing further haemorrhages from a failure. That is on the assumption the market as a whole is still healthy. The other problem is spotting when the market is sick and likely to get worse, knowing whether it is a blip or the market on the turn.

For instance, there is the time when a roaring bull market suddenly falters. This could be the result of some external trigger like a trade war – though why the hurricane that roared across southern England in October 1987 should have triggered a plunge in prices still leaves market analysts baffled. Another cause can be a general loss of impetus. In some curious and indefinable way the enthusiasm that had buoyed up everybody and had seemed ready to continue forever suddenly drains away. Nothing seems really satisfying. Even good news fails any longer to lift prices, though unhappy news knocks them back. These are signals of a market on the turn and a time to start selling before the rout starts.

Once the bear market is truly under way, selling on the way down is trickier. Professional investors are ruthless about getting out if the signs look bad, and many institutions now have computer programs that automatically start selling when a certain percentage decline has been noted. This is one of the reasons the New York stock exchanges can sometimes register accelerating falls in a share or even the market as a whole, as computers are automatically triggered to save what can be salvaged. Private shareholders, however, are always slow to sell. It is reckoned to be a mixture of ignorance (they have not been following the shares' performance), sentimental attachment to a carefully chosen share, and a sort of inertia that suggests hanging on for just another day or so in case it bounces back.

The judgement is between cutting your losses and not missing out on a recovery. There are some warning signals that may suggest a discreet exit. For instance, there are conflicting indicators and rumours about the company. Another good test is to ask oneself whether the shares have become so low and the indications of good profits so convincing that the shares seem an irresistible bargain – if not, it is probably a good idea to sell. Even if you are convinced the market has got it wrong and the business will bounce back, it can be shrewd to sell. Then, if the price continues to fall and the indications are coming through that the company has turned the corner, you can always get back in.

27 | Tax

Tax is always complicated, and huge manuals have been written on how to get the best deal possible to frustrate the efforts of the Inland Revenue. This chapter merely skims the surface.

Governments have tried to steer us towards some investment vehicles by tax incentives because they think it will be good for us or for the country. It would be foolish not to take advantage of any extra benefits provided by the taxman, but it would be just as silly to invest purely for the tax break. This is especially so as the management fees for some schemes need careful scrutiny to test whether the deal is still worth it after the professionals have had their share of the cream. So weigh the alternatives and go for the one that is best by your personal criteria and only go for the savings in tax if the investment would have made sense without them.

Governments are also good at taking money off us. So there is not only tax on getting into shares – stamp duty – but also on the benefits from most kinds of investment, both on the income and on the capital appreciation. Dividends, including scrip issues and bonus shares, count as income and are therefore subject to income tax. Most companies pay dividends net of tax.

The Inland Revenue publishes some useful booklets on tax, including one on capital gains, available from all tax offices.

ISAs

Individual Savings Accounts are part of the social engineering attempted by governments to persuade us to save more of our income by providing tax incentives. There are three broad categories of destinations for the money: deposit accounts at banks, building societies and National Savings; investment-linked insurance plans; and stock market investments such as shares, unit trusts, bonds, futures, options, gilts, etc, with at least five years life left to them.

A mini-ISA invests in one of these; a maxi-ISA must have the stock market content plus either or both of the others. These schemes are then managed by a designated business and for each tax year you can have one maxi-ISA manager though any number of managers for mini-ISAs. It is this management that is casting a shadow over the scheme, since some managers charge enough to outweigh the tax benefits.

DIVIDENDS

Dividends on shares are almost invariably paid net of tax and the voucher that comes with the payment notification contains details of a tax credit. People who do not normally pay income tax cannot reclaim the tax already paid on the dividend, and people paying tax at the basic rate need pay no further tax on the income. But people paying tax at the higher rate have to pay at 32½ per cent of the gross, though the credit detailed in the slip is set off against this. This complicated way of describing things, characteristic of the tax authorities, means in effect that about a quarter of the net dividend is due in tax for higher-rate payers.

So, for instance, someone owning 400 shares in Quilp & Heep Intercontinental, which pays a 15p dividend, would get a cheque for £60. Since the tax credit is 10 per cent, this represents 90 per cent of the gross dividend that would have therefore been £66.66 (60/90 x 100). As a result the tax credit notified with the cheque would be £6.66. Payers at the standard rate are then all square, but payers at the higher rate, obliged to pay 32½ per cent of the gross, must now calculate 66.66 x 32.5/100, which works out at £21.66. Setting off the £6.66 already paid leaves a liability of £15 to be sent to the Revenue.

Scrip issues of shares in lieu of dividend are treated in a similar way. There is no tax for people on the standard rate, and the higher rates are assumed to have had a 10 per cent tax credit.

If the company buys back shares the money received is treated as a dividend – covered by income tax, not capital gains tax.

CAPITAL PROFITS

A profit on the sale of shares is liable to tax for profits above the basic tax-free allowance. This is a pretty handsome chunk as far as most small investors are concerned. Capital gains tax is a problem only for people dealing in largish amounts or who have really struck it lucky with one of their stocks. In other words if the profit is so great that CGT is due you have done so well that a bit for the Exchequer seems less painful. Windfall shares received from demutualized building societies or insurance companies are counted as having cost nothing and anything made from their sale is counted as a capital gain, unless they have been put into a tax-sheltered scheme such as a PEP or ISA.

There is a tapered tax relief however, so holding shares for a long time will reduce the tax liability. If the shares were bought before April 1998 the price rise can be adjusted for inflation before tax is payable. Dealing costs in buying and selling are allowable against the total gain, there is also an allowance for part-paid shares, and gifts between spouses are tax-free, so the portfolio can be adjusted to net the maximum allowance.

Unquoted shares are a problem since there is no publicly available unequivocal price for dealing. For these deals you will just have to haggle with the local tax office (but see also the tax advantages of Aim investments, which count as unquoted, in Chapter 20).

As is only fair, losses made from selling shares in the same tax year can be set off against the profit. And if any of the companies actually go bust, the shares are reckoned to have been sold at that date for nothing and the capital loss from the purchase price can also be set off against gains.

All this may help with decisions between alternative courses of buying and selling, though once again being guided purely by tax differences is usually a mistake. A good accountant can advise on such things at a relatively low cost.

SHARE SCHEMES

Receiving shares from an employer counts as pay and so is subject to income tax. If the employee (and that includes directors) buys the shares at a discount to the market price, the discount portion is the bit on which tax is paid.

Under approved profit-sharing schemes the company can allocate tax-free shares to workers, though as you would expect there is a raft of rules about the details. Share option schemes that meet all the Chancellor's requirements have few advantages.

TAX INCENTIVES TO RISK

The government wants innovations to be financed, high technology to get started, and new ideas to be given a chance. Investment institutions such as venture capitalists will not touch them, so the tax incentives are directed at private investors. These are risky ventures and though rewards can be high for a success, the chance of failure is also pretty high. Even with the tax come-ons this is an area for people with a steady base of safe investment who also have a few hundred thousand to gamble with.

Enterprise Investment Schemes

Investment in newly issued shares of an unlisted company can be set off against income tax at a reduced rate, but the full relief both in income and capital gains taxes comes only if the shares are held for years. Losses can be set off against either capital gains or income. Capital gains tax can also be deferred by rolling the investment over: after selling the fruits of one successful punt you can put the proceeds into another similar venture and the tax is not due until the cash is eventually realized.

Enterprise Zone Trusts

This is more an incentive to provide commercial property for budding businesses and so falls outside the scope of this book.

Venture capital trusts

This is really just a collective version of the Enterprise Investment Scheme. The tax breaks are similar but the investment is into a quoted financial vehicle, which in turn puts the cash into a range of entrepreneurial businesses. This means the risk is reduced, as with investment and unit trusts, by spreading the money over a number of ventures.

TAX RATES

Chancellors have to seem to be earning their keep, so every year's budget produces some tinkering with tax rates, allowances and incentives. Sometimes impending elections or other political exigencies produce a need for other public reactions as well. As a result, the picture continuously shifts in detail. That is why this chapter has given a general picture and the overall policies but largely omitted numbers. To get the latest levels of tax rates, allowances and benefits, telephone any of the 10 largest accountancy firms, all of which will almost certainly have a free leaflet summarizing the current position.

Useful addresses

American Stock Exchange, www.amex.com
Association of Investment Trust Companies, 8 Chiswell Street, London EC1Y 4YY, tel: 020 7282 5555, www.aitc.co.uk
Association of Private Client Investment Managers and Stockbrokers, 112 Middlesex Street, London E1 7HY, tel: 020 7247 7080, www.apcims.co.uk (represents most of the private client stockbrokers plus a large number of other investment managers)
Association of Unit Trusts and Investment Funds, 65 Kingsway, London WC2B 6TD, tel: 020 7831 0898, www.investmentfunds.org.uk
Banking Ombudsman, 70 Gray's Inn Road, London WC1X 8NB, tel: 0345 660902
Bloomberg news agency (also share prices), www.bloomberg.co.uk
Cantrade Investments, 4 Chiswell Street, London EC1Y 4UP
Carol, www.carol.co.uk
Chart Analysis, tel: 020 7439 4961
Chartered Institute of Taxation, 12 Upper Belgrave Street, London SW1X 8BB, tel: 020 7235 9381
Chase de Vere Investments, Lincoln's Inn Fields, London WC2A 3JX, tel: 0800 985 9000, fax: 01225 445744, www.chasedevere.co.uk
City Wire, www.citywire.co.uk
Companies House, www.companieshouse.gov.uk
Crown Way, Cardiff CF4 3UZ, tel: 01222 388588
37 Castle Terrace, Edinburgh EH1 2EB
55 City Road, London EC1, tel: 020 7253 9393
Ethical Investments Research Service, 504 Bondway Business Centre, 71 Bondway, London SW8 1SQ
European Investor (which also carries reports from the Blue Sky surveys), www.europeaninvestor.com

Financial Services Authority, 25 The North Colonnade, London E14 5HS, tel: 020 7676 1000, www.fsa.gov.uk

Hargreaves Lansdown (stockbrokers), 4 Brighton Mews, Clifton BS8 2NX, tel: 0117 900 9000, fax:0117 973 9902

Hemmington Scott Publishing, 26 Whiskin Street, London EC1R 0JD, tel: 020 7278 7769, fax: 020 7278 9808, www.hemscott.net

Hong Kong Stock Exchange, www.sehk.com.hk

Interactive Investor International, www.iii.co.uk

Investment Research, Cambridge, tel: 01223 356251

Investments Ombudsman, 6 Fredericks Place, London EC2R 8BT, tel: 020 7796 3065

Investors Compensation Scheme, Cotton Centre, Cotton Lane, London SE1 2QB, tel: 020 7367 6000

London International Financial Futures & Options Exchange, Cannon Bridge, London EC4R 3XX, tel: 020 7623 0444, fax: 020 7588 3624, www.liffe.com

London Stock Exchange, 10 Paternoster Square, London EC4 7LS, tel: 020 7797 1000, www.londonstockexchange.com

Moneyfacts, North Walsham, Norfolk NR28 0BD, tel: 01692 500765

The Motley Fool, www.fool.co.uk

Nasdaq, www.nasdaq.com

New York Stock Exchange, www.nyse.com

Primark-Extel, 1 Mark Square, London EC2A 4EG, tel: 020 7566 1910, fax: 020 7566 1911

Proshare, 13 Basinghall Street, London EC2V 5HU, tel: 020 7394 5200, fax: 020 7600 0947, www.proshare.org.uk

Tokyo Stock Exchange, www.tse.or.jp/eindex.html

Tradepoint, www.tradepoint.co.uk

Vancouver Stock Exchange, www.vse.ca

Some execution-only stockbrokers

James Brearley & Sons, tel: 01253 21474
Durlacher, tel: 020 7628 4306
First Direct, tel: 0345 100100
Gall & Eke, tel: 0161 237 9443

Hargreaves Lansdowne, tel: 0117 980 9800
Henderson Crossthwaite, tel: 0345 125719
Lloyds Bank, tel: 0345 888100
Walter Lunniss & Co, tel: 01603 622265
NatWest, tel: 020 7895 5018
Albert E Sharpe, tel: 0121 200 2244
Charles Stanley & Co, tel: 020 7739 8200
Walker Crips Weddle Beck, tel: 020 7253 7502

Some online stockbrokers

Barclays, www.barclays-stockbrokers.co.uk
James Brearley, www.brearley.co.uk
Cave & Sons, www.caves.co.uk
Comdirect (a German broker), www.comdirect.de
Consors (French broker), www.consors.fr
CPR E*Trade (French broker), www.cprbourse.tm.fr
DLJ Direct, www.dljdirect.co.uk
ebanking.com (Belgian broker), www.ebanking.com
E-Cortal, www.e-cortal.com
E*Trade, www.etrade.co.uk
Fastrade, www.torrie.co.uk
Fortis Ebanking, www.fortis.com
Goy Harris Cartwright, www.ghcl.co.uk
Halifax Share Dealing, www.halifax.co.uk/sharedealing
Hargreaves Lansdown Stockbrokers,
www.hargreaveslansdown.co.uk
Keytrade (Belgian broker), www.keytrade.com
Killik & Co, www.killik.co.uk
Mybroker, www.mytrack.com
Quick & Reilly (US broker), www.quickandreilly.com
Redmayne, www.redmayne.co.uk
Charles Schwab (UK offshoot of US broker),
www.schwab-europe.com
SelfTrade (French broker), www.selftrade.com
The Share Centre, www.share.co.uk
Sharelink, www.sharelink.co.uk

Sharepeople, www.sharepeople.co.uk
Stocktrade, www.stocktrade.co.uk
Sure Trade, www.suretrade.com
Swiss Netbanking (Swiss broker)
Torrie & Co, www.torrie.co.uk
T D Waterhouse, www.tdwaterhouse.co.uk
Xest, www.xest.com

Services for investment clubs

Barclays
DLJ Direct
Hargreaves Lansdown
NatWest
Charles Schwab
Share Centre
T D Waterhouse

Glossary

acid test – see Chapter 15; a check on the company's balance sheet to see if it has liquid assets to meet its current debts

Alternative Investment Market – the part of the London Stock Exchange for small companies or ones too young to meet the requirements for full quotation; often abbreviated to Aim

assets – net assets in the balance sheet are defined as capital plus reserves, or total assets minus current liabilities, less the long-term creditors

authorized share capital – every company has a memorandum and articles of association which show how many shares it may issue. It is not compelled to issue all of them and many companies keep some in reserve for rights issues, employee incentives and the like (see also issued share capital)

bear market – a time of generally falling share prices

bid – the price at which the managers of unit trusts will buy back the units from investors, compared with the offer at which they sell units; also loosely used for the offer in a takeover

blue chip – a top-quality company and its shares, derived from the top-value gaming chips used in casinos and poker

bond – a tradeable fixed-interest security (eg gilts, debentures)

bonus issue – another name for a scrip issue; the distribution of shares to existing holders at no cost to them

broker – see stockbroker

bull market – a period of rising share prices

common stock – the US term for ordinary shares

convertible – a class of paper issued by companies (such as loan stock or preference shares) that can be converted into ordinary shares at a preset price, and usually on a set date

coupon – the interest rate on a corporate bond; it comes from the practice in the past of attaching to the certificate a series of little coupons that one had to clip off and send to the company to collect the interest

Crest – the stock exchange's electronic register of share owner-ship to replace paper certificates (see Chapter 19)

dividend – it is stated as so much per share, so a company declar-ing a dividend of 12p pays that amount to the holder of every share on issue. The owner of 1,000 shares would get a cheque for £12, minus tax

dividend cover – see Chapter 15

dividend yield – see Chapter 15

Easdaq – European Association of Security Dealers Automated Quotation system, was a pan-European stock market based on the Nasdaq, but has since merged with it

equities – another name for ordinary shares

Eurotop – an index encompassing Europe's top 100 and 300 companies

exceptional items – profits or losses in the company accounts from dealings that are not part of the company's main trading, such as the sale of a factory

ex-dividend – a share being sold soon after a dividend has been declared with the seller still getting the payment

flotation – bringing a company to the stock market to get its shares publicly traded

FTSE 100 – stock market index covering the 100 companies with the largest market capitalization. Since companies grow or shrink, become fashionable or are suddenly shunned, the con-stituents of the index change continually. As a result it is an indication of the temper of the market as a whole rather than of the performance of any specific set of companies

fundamental analysis – looking at the company behind the share, as opposed to technical analysis, which looks at only the changes in share prices; it involves calculating net asset value and probable future dividends, which may involve economic predictions as well

gearing – in balance sheets a ratio of a company's borrowings to its equity

gilts – short for gilt-edged, the usual name for government-issued bonds

hedging – protecting against a potential liability

insider – somebody with privileged access to information about a company, such as directors; it is illegal to trade in shares on such knowledge

IPO – initial public offering; the US term for flotation

issued share capital – these are the shares the company has actually sold as opposed to the authorized share capital that it is allowed to sell

Jiway – a joint venture between US merchant bank Morgan Stanley and Swedish software company OM Gruppen to create a stock market dealing in US, Swedish, British and German shares (see Chapter 20)

leverage – the US term for gearing

Liffe – London International Financial Futures and Options Exchange (pronounced 'life'); the 'options' part was a later addition, after the initials had become a well-known acronym

liquidation – the sale of an insolvent company's assets to pay creditors

liquidity – one meaning is a measure of how easy it is to buy or sell the shares – how many shares are available, how many people trade in them, how great is the volume of dealings; it is also used to assess assets by how readily they can be turned into cash: the more readily, the more liquid they are

London Stock Exchange – the largest stock exchange operating in Britain

market correction – a fall in share prices

members – the shareholders of a company

Nasdaq – National Association of Securities Dealers Automated Quotation system; New York-based electronic stock market with a heavy emphasis on companies using advanced technology

net asset value – all the assets of a company minus all its liabilities and capital charges (see Chapter 15)

Neuer Markt – Frankfurt-based market for shares of smaller, younger companies than are normally admitted to the main stock exchange

nominee account – shares held by an institution or company on behalf of individual shareholders (see Chapter 22)

Ofex – contraction of off-exchange; a computerized stock market run by market-maker J P Jenkins, founded in 1995. It has about 200 companies, generally small, that are either ineligible for or uninterested in the Alternative Investment Market

offer – the price at which managers of unit trusts sell the units to the public – it is higher than the bid price at which they are prepared to buy them back, and the difference is the spread

open ended – an investment vehicle that issues paper in ratio to the amount of investment it receives from the public; unit trusts (called mutual funds in the United States); there is no secondary market in the paper, so buying and selling is only with the management company

pound-cost averaging – accumulating a holding by investing the same amount of pounds in the securities at intervals; you get more shares for the money when the price is falling and that reduces the average cost per share

preferred stock – US term for preference shares

price/earnings ratio – this compares the current price of the share with the attributable earnings per share. It is the way the market compares expected growth in a company's dividend with the required rate of return by an investor. The formula says the correct price equals the expected current dividend, divided by the required return and expected growth in the company's dividends. So if the dividend now is 10p per share and this is expected to grow by 5 per cent a year but the current demand is for a return of 8 per cent, the calculation is $10/(0.08 - 00.5)$, which would make the right share price 333p.

put option – the right to sell a share at a set price within the period of the agreement

registrar – the organization that maintains the record of a company's shares and their ownership; run by specialist registrar companies, most of them are owned by major banks

re-rating – a change of opinion by the stock market; a surge of good news, a series of analysts' reports, the promise of wonderful new products and the like may make investors feel the company's prospects are better than the price rises, with a corresponding rise in the price/earnings ratio and fall in the yield. And conversely the other way

reserves – the non-distributed profits of a company, plus profits from revaluing assets, plus any share premium; this is not money in the bank but is used in the business, though it remains part of the shareholders' funds

return on capital – see Chapter 15

rights issues – one way a company raises money is by selling more shares, and sometimes it does this by giving the people who already own its shares the right of first refusal in proportion to the shares they already own

rule of 20 – a way of judging the euphoria or gloom of the market as a whole. It says the price/earnings ratio plus the inflation rate should equal 20

Seaq – stands for Stock Exchange Automated Quotations and is the electronic system that displays the bid and offer prices for securities by market makers, together with the size of the parcel they will deal in. The system shows the best price and the market makers are obliged to deal at the prices they display

SEATS Plus – a trading system used for Aim stocks and also for other shares without enough market-makers to create a competitive market; the computer screen shows any market-makers' prices plus orders from buyers and sellers seeking a counter-party

Sets – stands for Stock Exchange Electronic Trading Service, which is a sign of the shift from the traditional market, which was a quote-driven service (where traders put up prices at which they will trade and the agents of investors decide among them), to an order-matching service (where people wanting to trade enter their requirements into the computer, which then tries to pair them off)

share premium – if the nominal value of a company's share is 20p but it issues them at 50p, the 30p difference is in the books as the share premium account

shareholders' funds – the assets of a company minus its liabilities; since the shareholders own the business, what is left ultimately belongs to them

short – going short means a dealer is committed to delivering shares he or she does not own; it is done in anticipation of a falling price

spread – the difference between the buying and selling price of a share or other asset

stockbroker – a professional dealer in securities who acts as an agent for investors

straddle – buying simultaneously a buy and a put option in a share with the same exercise price and expiry date: a technique in options trading used by investors who expect volatility in the price of the underlying shares; it widens the break-even point but means they can make money if there is a substantial movement in either direction

support – in chartism it is the level at which falling prices stop or bounce because buyers are being tempted back

techMARK – the collection of technology-based companies quoted on the London Stock Exchange into a single index

technical analysis – in practice another name for the chartist way of looking at the market; it uses not just the conventional method of having a line to depict price movements, but also the 'point and figure' charts

Virt-X – a company (itself traded on the Alternative Investment Market) providing an electronic market in shares

volatility – the amount of fluctuation in a share price; the more it moves the greater the risk

warrants – a type of investment allowing the holder to buy paper from the issuer at a fixed price, sometime in the future; most are listed on the stock exchange and can be traded like any other investment, prior to their expiry date (see Chapter 2)

with-profits policy – an insurance cover that guarantees a payment at the end of the set term or on death, but which also adds an annual and a terminal bonus, the size of which depends on the company's profit; that in turn is affected mainly by its investment in shares

yield – is calculated by taking the amount of a dividend as a percentage of the current share price. So if the shares stand at 120p (irrespective of what the nominal price might be) a dividend of 12p represents a yield of 10 per cent. If the following day the shares drop to 100p, the yield will have correspondingly risen to 12 per cent. It is listed in the newspaper as yield and compares directly with what can be got in a bank or building society for the money, but should be higher

Further reading

Trying to produce a list for further reading is a deeply frustrating exercise. Hundreds of books are published every year for this type of use, ranging from explanations of technical or fundamental analysis that require an advanced degree in mathematics, through private winning systems, to dozens of laymen's guides on every aspect. It is because they usually fail to help a novice over the initial hurdles or to explain in plain English that this book was originally written. There are a few books around which may help, however, for people who want to delve deeper.

Books

Andrew, John (1993) *How to Understand the Financial Press*, Kogan Page, London

Ball, Adrian (1989) *Making Money from Penny Shares & Small Company Investments*, Kogan Page, London

Becket, Michael (1998) *An A to Z of Finance: A jargon-free guide to investment and the City*, Kogan Page, London

Berger, D, Gardner, D and Gardner, T (1998) *The Motley Fool Investment Guide*, Boxtree

Brett, Michael (1987, 1989, 1991) *How to Read the Financial Pages*, Business Books

Burke, Andrew (1999) *Market Speculating*, Rowton Press

Chancellor, Edward (1999) *Devil Take the Hindmost: A history of financial speculation*, Pan

Cohen, David (2000) *Bears & Bulls: The psychology of the stock market*, Metro

Davidson, Alexander (2000) *How to Win in a Volatile Stock Market: The definitive guide to investment bargain hunting*, Kogan Page, London

Dixon, H (2000) *The Penguin Guide to Finance*, Penguin

Drury, T *Investment Clubs: The low-risk way to stock market profits*, Rushmere Wynne

Eckett, Stephen (1997) *Investing Online*, Pitman

Fisher, Philip (1996) *Common Stocks and Uncommon Profits*, Wiley

Gasking, T (1991) *How to Master Finance*, Business Books

Gill, J O (1990) *How to Understand Financial Statements*, Kogan Page, London

Goodson, M and Berger, D (1999) *The Fool's Guide to Investment Clubs*, Boxtree

Graham, B (1997) *The Intelligent Investor*, 4th edn, HarperCollins

Gray, B (1993) *Beginners' Guide to Investment*, 2nd edn, Random House

Hall, A D (1992, 1994, 1997) *Getting Started in Stocks*, Wiley

Harrison, D (2001) *The First Time Investor*, 2nd edn, Prentice-Hall,

Holmes, G and Sugden, A (1979, 1982, 1986, 1990, 1994) *Interpreting Company Accounts*, Woodhead Faulkner

International Labour Office (1966, 1985) *How to Read a Balance Sheet*, International Labour Office

Jennings, M (1994) *Better Money Management*, Piatkus

Keasey, K, Hudson, R and Littler, K (1998) *The Intelligent Guide to Stock Market Investment*, Wiley

Leach, R (1988) *Make Money on the Stock Exchange: A step by step guide through the system and sound advice to make you a winner*, Foulsham

Levinson, M (1999, 2000) *A Guide to Financial Markets*, The Economist

Lowe, J (1998, 2000) *The Which Guide to Shares*, Penguin

Lynch, P (1994) *Beating the Street*, Simon & Schuster

Malkiel, B (1973, 1975, 1981, 1985, 1990) *A Random Walk Down Wall Street*, Norton

Markman, J D (2001) *Online Investing*, 2nd edn, Microsoft Press

Millard, B (1993, 1998) *Winning on the Stock Market*, Wiley

Nursaw, W (1963, 1966, 1967) *The Art and Practice of Investment*, Hutchinson

O'Connor, G (1996) *A Guide to Stockpicking*, Random House

Parker, R H (1972, 1982, 1988) *Understanding Company Financial Statements*, Penguin

Pendlebury, M and Groves, R (1990) *Company Accounts*, Unwin Hyman

Reid, W and Middleton, D R (1971, 1992) *The Meaning of Company Accounts*, Gower

Ryland, P (1997, 1998, 2000) *Pocket Investor*, The Economist

Scott, M (2000) *The UK Guide to Online Brokers*, Scott

Slater, J (1994) *How to Use Company REFS: A guide to really essential financial statistics*, Hemmington Scott

Slater, J (1997) *The Zulu Principle*, Orion

Smith, T (1996) *Accounting for Growth: Stripping the camouflage from company accounts*, 2nd edn, Random House

Temple, P (2001) *Traded Options: A private investor's guide*, London International Financial Futures and Options Exchange, London

Vaitilingam, R (1993) *Guide to Using the Financial Press*, FT Pitman

Vause, B (1997) *Guide to Analysing Companies*, The Economist

Warren, R (1988, 1990) *How to Understand and Use Company Accounts*, Hutchinson

The Shareholder Action Handbook
The Investor's Guide to Information Sources, ProShare
Attractive Perks for UK Shareholders, Hargreaves Lansdown
Barclays – Investment Study
How to Buy and Sell Shares, London Stock Exchange, London
ISA Guide, Chase de Vere Investments
Annual Smaller UK Companies Handbook, Financial Times
FT Extel Major Companies Handbook, Primark-Extel
UK Smaller Companies Handbook

Magazines

Bloomberg Money
Internet Investor
Investor
Investors Chronicle
Investors Week
Money Management
Money Marketing
Money Observer
Moneywise
Shares
What Investment
Your Money
Your Pension

Index

Page reference in *italics* indicate figures.

Index of advertisers